The Elusive Obvious
The Science of Non-verbal Communication

Michael Grinder

Author of *Managing Groups* and
Charisma—The Art of Relationships

with Mary Yenik

Dedication

To Gail

The Elusive Obvious is the science of non-verbal communication. The science provides the stepping stones to the art of communication.

While writing this book, Gail and I were browsing in an art gallery. I kept eyeing one particular bronze sculpture. As I drifted back to the same piece a third time, the proprietor sidled over to me and whispered, "If you are wondering whether to purchase, just know that 'art is what you can't live without'." I immediately looked over at Gail and realized that she was my only true art piece.

Acknowledgments

The good Lord provided me with certain abilities; writing has come late to me in life. I sincerely thank the whole village for sharing their talents in critiquing, expanding, revising and producing this work. Special recognition goes to Rudolf Schulte-Pelkum for his diligence in helping us with the formatting and final editing of this book.

Holly Adams, Luke Aitken, Susan Albert, Richard and Pam Anderson, Laura Arellano, Isabel Azevedo, Rachel Babbs, Bob Beck, Diane Bergeron, Carla Bettens, Jodi Buchanan, Ron Burnett, Michael Cahill, Phil Callero, Kathryn Carter, Laura Cervantes, Regan Chandler-Nelson, Alexander Christiani, Kathy Coffin, Tony Cummins, Grace Marie Curtin, Charles Damerell, Theresa David, Krista Dettloff, Ellen Dietrich, Gabriele Dolke, Tom Dotz, Jeff Dulcich, Pam Dunnick, Pat Duran, Jill Dutchess, Jenny Edwards, Sabine Eichenmeuller, Sabine Emmerz, Joan Engle, Linda Fitch, Chrissy Free, Lynda Fudold, Kaze Gadway, Emily Garfield, Denise Gerrard, Mary Gibson, Eric Goodman, Amanda Gore, Gail Grinder, Leticia Guttierez, Linda Haines, Tim Hallbom, Tom Heaney, Paul Henderson, Gill Hicks, John Hicks, Janet Horn, Wayne Hunnicut, Shirley Jallad, Kris Janati, Matt Jensen, Monica Jonsson, Mark Jordan, Brooke Kerns, Diane Kizler, Dennis Kobelin, Lauren Kuhn, Liana Lafranier, Alison Lally, Barbara and Michael Lawson, Ilene Levy, Wolfgang Linker, Hazel-Ann Lorkins, April Luttman, Anita MacLeod, Greg Meyer, Cindy Miesbach, Rick Mullins, Archie Mundegar, Mary Mustoe, Margie Nelson, Toy Odiakosa, Karrie Olson, Joyce Patterson, Charlotte Pennye, Jane Peterson, Gary Phillips, Connie Portele, Jon Potter, Cherry Potts, Carol Powles, Jeff Reed, Joe Rodriguez, Andrea Rohmert, Vincent Samatowic, Sharon Sayler, Hans Schneider, Rudolf Schulte-Pelkum, Chuck Sester, Tracy Sinclair, Curtis Smith, Suzi Smith, Bill Sommers, Eddi Sowa, Sarah Spilman, John Steinberg, Nancy Stout, Kathryn Tochtrop, Scott Turner, Kate Warren, Elaine Wetherup, Diane Williams, Rick Williams, Graham Wilson, Gail and Lou Woodford, Mary Yonek, Mary Yenik, Dianne Yonker, Kendall Zoeller and Steve Zuieback.

Additional Acknowledgment

The title of this book is the same as a fine work by Moshe Feldenkrais. This is not by accident. I was first introduced to Moshe's approach to body alignment in the 1970s. There is a lot to movement. What is elusive to the person doing the movement is obvious to the trained Feldenkrais observer. And while this paragraph can't do justice to the entirety of Moshe's work, I trust that my own admiration of, and benefit from his discoveries, is a form of flattery.

The Cover Design and Layout Assistance: Sharon Sayler, webmaster@michaelgrinder.com

Desktop Publishing: Stout Graphics, Nancy Stout, nkstout@comcast.net

Pentimento is a trademark owned by Michael Grinder & Associates.
ISBN: 978-1-883407-13-1

The Elusive Obvious—The Science of Non-verbal Communication can be purchased directly from:
Michael Grinder & Associates
16303 NE 259th Street
Battle Ground, WA 98604
(360) 687-3238; FAX (360) 687-0595
Website: www.michaelgrinder.com

Second Edition 2009, Third Edition 2013

Table of Contents

To be respectful of gender equality and yet provide the reader with a fluid reading style, the sections of the book alternate the female and male pronoun usage. At the bottom of each section's first page, the gender pronouns for that section are explained.

Introduction

In the movie *Karate Kid*, a young teenager is about to be hassled by some adolescents when an elderly man rescues him. It is obvious to the lad that the senior citizen is a master with self-defense abilities. What is elusive is how he gained such skills. The grateful lad seeks the martial artist's mentorship. Having gained agreement, the eager pupil arrives on the appointed day for his first lesson; however, the master has him wax the many automobiles on his car lot. Over and over, the eager pupil moves his arms in a circular motion. Disappointed that he will have to delay the start of his learning, he obediently polishes the vehicles. Having finished the job, he bounces over to the master's house—only to learn he must now paint the fence. He is instructed to stroke the brush up and down with the wrist bending in a specific manner. By the time the fence is dutifully done, the lad's disappointment has turned to resentment. He approaches the master and vents his anger at not being taught the craft he sought.

The martial artist makes an attacking swing toward the pupil who, without thinking, does the swirling movement of the wax job and blocks the attack. This response is countered by an aggressive frontal lunge by the master. Much to the student's surprise, he automatically thwarts the advance with the stroking action of the fence painting. The master has proven that the two dull chores have

---

To be respectful of gender equality and yet provide the reader with a fluid reading style, in this section through the start of Chapter One the communicator is referred to by male pronouns and other people are referred to by female pronouns.

value—benefits that were obvious to the master but elusive to the pupil.

So, too, *The Elusive Obvious* contains two parts: the "Pentimento" (21 non-verbal patterns of communication) and "How Not To Get Shot." Pentimento reveals the underlying foundation of non-verbal communication. How Not To Get Shot is the most popular application of the Pentimento patterns. By understanding and practicing each skill from the Pentimento and How Not To Get Shot until they become natural and habitual—the communicator's version of waxing cars and painting fences—the reader will acquire the behavioral skills of a master communicator. By learning this powerful combination of skills, the reader will have a dependable way to handle volatile situations while preserving relationships. Collectively, the Pentimento and How Not To Get Shot comprise the Science of Non-verbal Communication.

Model of Professional Development

While we have heard the expression, "the art and science of communication," in reality they are learned in the reverse sequence. Like the impulsive young student in *Karate Kid*, we are drawn to the magic of the Art but what we truly need is daily practice in the discipline of the Science. The Science of Communication must be learned first if we are to reach the Art of Communication.

A closer examination reveals that we go through two stages of the Science and two stages of the Art as we advance in our careers.

The four levels of professional development are:

Receptivity: permission—the "if"
Perception: timing—the "when" } = **Art**

Process: the non-verbal level—the "how"
Content: the verbal level—the "what" } = **Science**

Science

The first two levels (content and process) of professional development deal with the Science of Communication. When a communicator is new to a position, discipline, industry, or culture, the person is internally oriented. On the content level of communication, the person is searching for the words to speak or, if listening, trying to understand *what* is being said. Once the person knows the *what* level of communication, she progresses to emphasizing *how* to deliver the *what*. This second stage of professional development—the process level of communication—involves learning and practicing the elements of non-verbal communication. *Non-verbal* factors, not verbal, are the major determinants of meaning in any communication.[1]

Art

Perception and receptivity comprise the two levels of the Art of Communication. Once a communicator knows the range of non-verbal behaviors she can use, the question becomes *when* to use the various behaviors.

For instance: at a meeting, if a communicator speaks and gestures with her elbows on the table, she will not command as much attention as if she speaks and gestures with her elbows off the table. Yet, if a communicator is speaking during an hour-long meeting, she may want to speak and gesture with her elbows on the table for most of the meeting. Then when she gets to the most important point(s), she takes her elbows off the table to increase the listeners' attention. By changing to more effective behaviors she marks off in the listeners' minds the point(s) she wants them to remember. Knowing when to take her elbows off the table is an example of the *when* (perception) level of communication.

The ultimate level of one's professional development in the Art and Science of Communication is receptivity. What is receptivity? With regards to an individual, we see openness, willingness to listen and consider, as well as positive expectations. With regards to a company we look for the positive effects of reputation, name recognition and public relations. Once this level is reached and maintained, communication becomes easier. Why? Each of the levels of professional development supersedes the previous level. For example, someone who is held in high esteem (receptivity) can be sloppy in delivering (process) a message and yet the message is more memorable than that same message delivered by an unknown person who has excellent non-verbal delivery.

Another example of permission superceding the previous levels is the research on medical malpractice. A doctor is not as likely to be sued if there is a positive relationship (i.e., permission) between the doctor and the patient.

Patterns of Pentimento

There are 21 non-verbal patterns of communication. They are collectively known as the Pentimento Patterns. The Italian word *pentimento* refers to an art process. When the surface of a painting cracks, what is beneath the surface is revealed (such as the original sketch marks or another painting). This process of revealing the substructure is called pentimento. We have borrowed this word from the world of art and transported it into the world of communication. By knowing the Pentimento Patterns—the hidden structure of communication—we can influence people with greater ease and elegance. The ability to influence people with ease and elegance is non-verbal intelligence.

> *The ability to influence people with ease and elegance is non-verbal intelligence.*

Benefits of Non-verbal Intelligence

Non-verbal intelligence is the ability to recognize, label, predict and (respond) to patterns of communication.

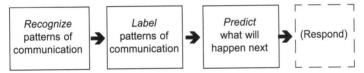

| Recognize patterns of communication | → | Label patterns of communication | → | Predict what will happen next | → | (Respond) |

Recognize

Most of us can recognize a variety of patterns. In fact, Charles Darwin asked Christian missionaries if they would be his eyes and ears to help him investigate what facial expressions were universal for Homo sapiens. They were able to stabilize seven facial expressions worldwide: anger, contempt, disgust, fear, happiness, sadness and surprise. For each facial expression, the missionaries identified the physical signs associated with it. For example, surprise is when the jaw drops down, upper eyelids are raised, eyebrows may be raised, and eyes widen. The characteristics of the other six emotions can be found in Paul Ekman's *Emotions Revealed.*

Label

If we can readily recognize certain basic non-verbal patterns of communication, what is the value of having a label for the pattern? It's valuable because it saves time and helps us remain objective; without a label, the mind becomes preoccupied with the pattern. For instance, suppose you are attending a meeting and a colleague begins to use a voice that is harsh and fast. Intuitively, you know that the colleague's switch to a harsh and fast voice is significant. Being able to label the voice as "anger" frees your perception to notice what is likely to happen next. The ability to label keeps us free of personal reactions.[2] Pentimento provides us with a label or vocabulary for non-verbal patterns.

> *Pentimento provides the vocabulary of non-verbal intelligence.*

Predict

The advantage of having labels for patterns of communication is that you can predict what is likely to happen next. By knowing the name of the pattern and having studied the pattern beforehand, you can also predict the effect it will have on others. It is on the predict level that the full value of Pentimento Patterns is realized because you are no longer surprised by what happens in a communication. This is important, because when we are surprised we lose our abilities. A person can have many laminated certificates on his wall, but all his degrees are for naught when he is surprised. Why? Because when surprised he breathes shallow. As a result, not enough oxygen gets to his brain and he can't think as well—brain freeze.

> *Surprise is the enemy of competence.*

(Respond)

Being able to predict and respond to non-verbal patterns is the Art of Communication. The title (Respond) is put in parentheses because the most artistic lesson you will learn is that it is okay to be unable to control what happens in a communication. Many humans finish their careers without ever having arrived at this level of non-verbal intelligence. They grow old never having come to terms with the reality that no matter how much they know or how hard they try to reach others, some people will remain unreceptive.

John Wooden, the most winning college basketball coach of all time never mentioned the word "win." He said that winning was the by-product of mastering the fundamentals of basketball. Like Wooden, the results we get are often the by-product of our skill—our artistry—in getting people to be *receptive* to our communication.

Note to the NLP Reader

(For those acquainted with neuro linguistic programming, this note is presented. For those who have never heard of NLP, feel free to be inquisitive.)

I was smart enough to be born into a fine family of nine children. Each of us contributes in a unique manner to the world. Brother John co-invented an approach called NLP. In fact, some of you might be reading this work because of my last name. Hopefully, by the time you finish reading this book, you will be familiar with my first name as well as my last name.

NLP offers the world many templates and axioms. One of my favorites is the notion that an excellent communicator has three perspectives:

- 1st perspective "Self"—knows where she is

- 2nd perspective "Other"—knows where the other is

- 3rd perspective "Fly"—knows what the situation looks like as seen by the "fly on the wall."

The ability to have three perspectives is especially critical in conflict-laden situations. The question is, how can she make sure that her "fly on the wall" is an accurate perspective instead of merely an extension of the "self," or (less likely) the "other" perspective? In the language of NLP, how does a communicator know if her fly on the wall perspective is free of distortions, deletions, and generalizations?

How can a communicator verify her own accuracy and objectivity? This work offers the following answer.

> *If a communicator can accurately predict the effect of a behavior, then she has an objective "fly on the wall" perspective.*

This work delineates the 21 basic non-verbal patterns of communication. The patterns are cross-culturally accurate. Amazingly, when they are used one can statistically predict the effect on the recipient. They meet the criterion of being the accurate fly on the wall. The study of the Pentimento gives an NLP practitioner that elusive third perspective—the fly on the wall perspective.

How to Use this Book

> *There is no magic, only magicians.*

As a company, Michael Grinder and Associates is committed to reversing the trend of over-training and under-implementing. To assist the reader in learning the skills in this work, the following features are included:

- **Shadow box**. The key sayings are in shadow boxes. Some readers like to surf pages to read the shadow boxes. Then when an idea intrigues them, they read the full text.

- **Vignettes.** Many of us learn best through stories. These are boxed and shown in a different font. Some readers will jump to them and when engaged will then read the text; others will read the text and use the vignettes for reinforcements. The Index lists the vignettes by title.

- [*Stage directions*]. The scenarios in this book indicate that the skills are practical and every day. Often these scenarios are presented in a play-like format. The stage directions of the non-verbals involved are in [*italics inside brackets*].

I-1

- *Free Worksheets*—All of the major concepts of the book are formatted into easy-to-use worksheets. These forms allow the reader the opportunity to practice the skills. A worksheet is indicated by a CD icon in the margin. The first number indicates the chapter followed by the worksheet number. For example, I-1 indicates Introduction, first worksheet. The free worksheets are downloadable at www.michaelgrinder.com

- **As a learner** (practice exercises). When you see the symbol of a runner, you are encouraged to engage in the learning activity. Reading this work and not doing the exercises is fine—it will increase your cognitive competence in non-verbal communication. Actually doing the exercises will increase your behavioral competence. So both the cognitive and behavioral readers are welcome and the latter will profit even more. The best way to incorporate these valuable skills into your professional lives is to form a cadre of learners who fax or email one worksheet to each other weekly. Since the Pentimento Patterns are always present, concentrate on one skill a week. This habit will allow you to incorporate that specific skill into your repertoire. Be patient with yourself.

> *Be ambitious enough to be patient.*
> *Practice one skill a week.*

- **Reference.** Chapters One through Five contain the 21 basic non-verbal patterns of communication. To increase the reader's fluidity of learning, marginal icons will unobtrusively refer to the pattern.

- **Bookmark**. This book includes a laminated bookmark with a summary of the 21 Pentimento patterns on one side and the 8 components of How Not to Get Shot! on the other side. This bookmark is a handy reference when attending meetings and events.

- **DVD**. Each Pentimento pattern and How Not to Get Shot! component is explained and demonstrated on 60 minutes of video footage. Available through the website.

- **Free Screensavers**. We are all very busy and yet want to continue to professionally grow. Screensavers address this need. When our computers are at rest, the concepts appear on the screen with an attractive background. The page reference is listed to encourage us to further extend our learning. Free downloads are available at www.michaelgrinder.com.

- **Flash Cards**. The twenty-one Pentimento patterns and eight How Not to Get Shot! components have been produced in a deck of full-color, plastic-coated cards (the size of a standard deck of playing cards). Each card highlights a different pattern or component with written explanations and accompanying illustrations. Their mobile size makes them great for use at important interactions and reinforcing the ideas you've been learning. (Created by Isabel Azevedo and Kari Kvaerner.) Available through the website.

If Your Time is Short

If you are teaching non-verbal communication and don't have time to become a complete student of the twenty-one patterns of communication, we recommend the following essential patterns:

   #1.   Points of Focus

   #4.   Voice Patterns: Credibility and Approachability

   #9.   Frozen Hand Gesture

 #21.   Pause and Look Intelligent

If you are involved with group dynamics, we recommend our programs in Group Dynamics, e.g., "Group Wizardry" and "Group Mastery Certification." (See our website for details: www.michaelgrinder.com.) In addition to the essential patterns, the patterns that are most critical for group dynamics are:

   #3.   Peripheral Sight

   #6.   ABOVE (Pause) Whisper

If you are interested in presentation skills, in addition to the above mentioned six patterns, we suggest:

   #2.   Transitions Between Points of Focus

   #8.   Decontamination

 #18.   Pause, Breathe and Join

 #19.   Break and Breathe

If you are interested in psychology, we suggest Breathing Patterns:

 #15.   BLIP (Breathing Level Indicates Permission)

 #16.   Indicators of Breathing

 #17.   Influencing Another's Breathing

Part One:

Patterns of Pentimento

Overview

As previously stated, in the world of fine art, the term *pentimento* refers to a special property of some oil paintings. Oil paints have linseed oil as a binder or glue to hold the paint pigment in place. The old master painters did not know that as dried linseed oil ages, certain colors of paint become increasingly transparent. Gradually, the underpainting and even the original pencil sketch marks become visible and show, in exquisite detail, the underlying structure of the painting. This revelation of the underlying structure of a painting is called *pentimento*. The following is an explanation of how the term *pentimento* is applied to the world of communication.

Models of Communication

When a person studies a model of communication, he often views the model as having multiple layers:

- Foundational philosophy. The basic components of the system and presuppositions upon which the work is based

- Strategies. The techniques, interventions, and patterns of behavior

- Refinements. The hands-on, how-to levels

A learner usually progresses from abstract to concrete, from general to specific.

The art world usage of pentimento describes what exists and yet is hidden from sight. The world of communication is similar to the world of art in that it, too, has an underlying structure, one that is always present but often hidden from the untrained eye. Even to the keen observer of communication patterns, the role of non-verbals is often elusive, even mysterious. This work reveals the non-verbals that form the foundation and influence the success of communication and once revealed the non-verbal patterns are obvious. Amazingly, this set of 21 non-verbals can be found at the heart of all popular communication models, no matter how different they appear on the surface.

Transactional Analysis, Thomas Harris. Foundational philosophy. People operate from three core personas: Child, Adult, and Parent.

Person A   **Person B**

(Parent)   (Parent)

(Adult)   (Adult)

(Child)   (Child)

Strategies. The practitioner is presented with various combinations of strategies that can occur between two people and learns how to avoid being judgmental or feeling like a victim (not OK positions—Examples One and Two), eventually progressing to the OK position of the "Adult" (Example Three).

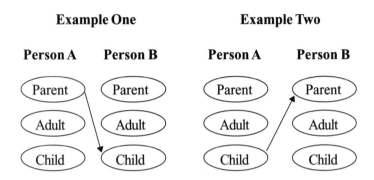

Refinements. Practitioner's goal is to eventually view both himself and the other person as "OK." "I'm OK, you're OK" is described as the Adult-Adult relationship.

Example Three

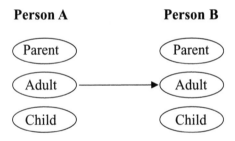

Principled Negotiations, Fisher and Ury

Two Harvard professors produced a series of books (*Getting to Yes, Getting Past No, Getting Together, Getting it Done*) based on the concept of win-win communication.

Foundational philosophy. Any conflict can be viewed from three levels: the issues involved, the motives/needs that are generating the parties' positions on the issues, and the relationship between the parties. The essence of successful negotiations involves creation of win-win results, taking care to preserve long-term relationships.

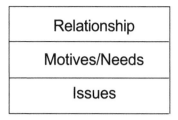

Strategies. The practitioner learns and practices the concepts of: BATNA (Best Alternative to The Negotiated Agreement), generating multiple options, separating people from the problems, distinguishing substantive issues, focusing on agreements, and communicating on the relationship level. If the other person is operating from a win-lose position, the strategy is to shift the person to realizing how it is in her best interest to view the situation from the motives/needs of all parties. Any lasting solutions will consider all parties' motives/needs. The more the parties communicate on the relationship level the more options are available.

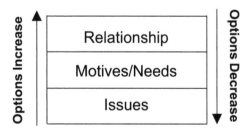

Refinements. The practitioner progresses to the following: being centered, using listening skills, establishing a constructive setting, and creating an appropriate feeling tone for the negotiation.

Neuro Linguistic Programming, Bandler and Grinder

Two people at the University of California Santa Cruz founded this model of communication.

Foundational philosophy. An effective communicator has four essential abilities: 1) rapport skills, 2) outcomes defined in sensory-specific detail, 3) acuity to notice results and 4) flexibility when communicating.

Strategies. The practitioner eventually learns to dovetail his outcomes with the other party's outcomes.

Refinements. The practitioner studies the subjective reality of the other person. This includes detecting her values, beliefs, and perceptual filters.

Cognitive Coaching, Costa and Garmston

Two professors who are well versed in thinking and questioning strategies established this template of communication.

Foundational philosophy. One's thinking can be influenced by questions and reflective thought increases success.

Strategies. The practitioner is immersed in strategies for identifying different kinds of conferences (i.e., coaching sessions) such as, for example, "planning" or "reflection." Questioning strategies are essential to send the client inside to reflect. The practitioner must have rapport with the client to ask the questions.

Refinements. The practitioner learns, among other things, to gauge a client's receptivity to coaching by noticing the client's breathing.

Refinement Level of Communication

The impression is that each model of communication (Transactional Analysis, Principled Negotiations, Neuro Linguistic Programming, Cognitive Coaching) is a complete system of thought. The shape of the pyramid gives the impression that practitioner has to master the wide foundation of each communication model in order to get to the top. The practitioner thinks it necessary to master the various layers within the model along the way, concentrating on this particular model to the exclusion of all others.

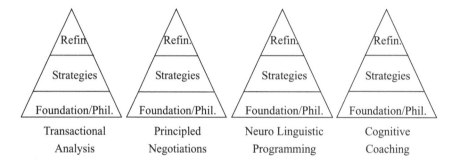

Transactional Analysis	Principled Negotiations	Neuro Linguistic Programming	Cognitive Coaching

It is as if the practitioner cannot easily transfer knowledge between the models; the practitioner finds it hard to utilize what he knows from one model when learning a new model.

The concept of Pentimento challenges this idea and asks the question, "Is there a fabric that weaves through every model?" If so, then what we learn by studying one model of communication might be readily transferable when studying another model.

The concept of Pentimento offers an alternative view of all models of communication. If the models of communication, as graphically represented by the pyramids, are turned and combined so that the sides of each model touch one another then an entirely different view is obtained.

In this hexagon the foundational philosophy, strategies, and refinements could be seen as rings of a circle. Two additional models have been added: Peter Senge's *Fifth Discipline* and Stephen Covey's *Seven Habits of Highly Effective People*. The circle refinements reveal the same set of micro skills—The Pentimento Patterns. By knowing the pentimento micro skills, every model of communication becomes easier to implement.

The refinement skills are the non-verbal ingredients of communication. Since there are a limited number of non-verbals, once we have a working understanding of these non-verbals skills, we can transfer the micro skills to all models of communication. Pentimento dissolves the illusion that each model of communication is a closed system by showing their underlying commonality.

For decades we have said that the non-verbal level of communication is more important than the verbal level so it makes sense that the non-verbals would be at the center of all communication.

Art and Science of Communication

So far, the communication models have been presented from the outside layers of foundational philosophy to the middle layers of strategies to the inner core of refinements. The top of each pyramid, the non-verbal layer, was the refinement level of that model of communication.

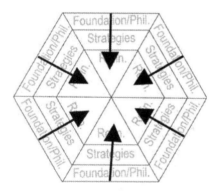

It is interesting to view the models of communication in the opposite direction. From this vantage point the non-verbals are not the refinements but the basis of all communication.

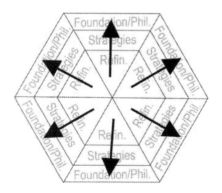

The Pentimento micro skills are the "how to" of all communication; the strategies are the selection and arrangement of certain micro skills. The foundational philosophy is where the macro intent of the communication is found. It is quite an enticement to realize that the Pentimento non-verbal skills are the micro means to accomplish the why of the macro level. The core is the fundamentals and the outer rings are the application.

At the risk of mixing metaphors, we move from painting to music. When a person is learning the piano the student is tasked to learn the keys and chords—the micro skills—before actual songs are experienced. Although the common parlance is the "Art and Science of piano...," in reality you are a scientist before you are an artist.

Simply stated, the Pentimento is the science (the keys and chords) that makes the practitioner of the different models of communication (the songs) an artist (the concert pianist).

The Pentimento paradigm offers us a way to explore models, skills, and strategies at their simplest, "bite size" chunk form for science learning. The Pentimento provides us with a blueprint to accelerate our growth to become artists of communication.

In addition to assisting people who are studying and implementing a specific model of communication, the Pentimento can be used for people who are not practitioners of a particular model. People read books because they seek guidance about real-life situations. Most books offer abstract goals of communication. They don't provide the specific details on how to get those goals. The books do a fine job of providing the macro level of guidance. These macro models provide the *why* of communication. In contrast, the Pentimento Patterns are the micro skills level that provides the *how* of the communication. You are encouraged to attend Pentimento trainings where you can become thoroughly versed in these invaluable micro level skills. We all have been raised with the saying,

> *"It's not what you say—it's how you say it."*

For the first time the Patterns of Pentimento explain this choreography of communication.

A metaphor from the world of sports may help us to understand and appreciate the value of the Patterns of Pentimento. The individual Pentimento skills are analogous to the fundamental skills like dribbling, running, passing, jumping, and shooting which Michael Jordan combines in an infinite variety of ways to dazzle basketball fans the world over. So too, effective communication is an infinite combination of what we do with our eyes, voice, body and breathing patterns.

> *"Execution is the chariot of genius."*
> William Blake

The Pentimento Patterns are the glossary of that execution. This work is committed to elevating the science of communication to a higher level, so that it can be accurately described as the discipline of communication. Since a discipline has its own language, the Pentimento creates terminology to distinguish one pattern from another. This book discusses 21 Pentimento Patterns. In examining the underlying structure of communication, the canvas of the macro models can be scratched to reveal the four categories of non-verbal communication:

Visual Patterns—what we do with our eyes; where we look

Auditory Patterns—what we do with our voice: intonation, pitch, speed, pausing

Kinesthetic Patterns—what we do with our body including gestures and locations

Breathing Patterns—what we do to regulate our breathing

Some clarification will increase our understanding of the patterns:

- Some of the patterns are found in more than one non-verbal category. For instance, the concepts of "Credibility" and "Approachability" are found not only in the auditory, but also in the visual and kinesthetic categories.

- Some of the patterns overlap from one category (e.g., visual) into another category (e.g., kinesthetic). "Eye and Hand Coordination" is an example of overlap. The more the overlap the more the skill approximates a strategy.

- The patterns are descriptions of behaviors, not of people.

- Out of necessity, the patterns might seem absolute, whereas they are intended to be the exaggerated ends of a behavioral continuum.

- The skills are not found in isolation but naturally clustered together and appearing in ever-changing patterns.[3]

As you study the patterns, it will become clear that breathing is the most important category. On the cover of the book the paintbrush that separates breathing from the visual, auditory and kinesthetic categories symbolizes the unique and paramount importance of breathing.

"In science, a model is superior when it can explain other models and not vice versa. Michael Grinder's Pentimento and Permission models not only combine other models but also explain *how to* get these models to work even better. He does this by delineating the ever-present but heretofore invisible non-verbal components of all communication. And while the visual, auditory and kinesthetic components have been known for some time, "Permission" properly categorizes them as manifestations of the quintessential[4] non-verbal breathing. Breathing is the only reliable indicator of permission, and what is even more provocative is that breathing is cross-culturally accurate."

Alexander Christiani[5]

Chapter 1

Visual Patterns

Overview

Visual non-verbal communication is what we do with our eyes. Research indicates that we take in more sensory information through our eyes than through our other senses. Our ability to control where we look is essential for effective communication.

There are three patterns:

- Pattern 1, Points of Focus—presents the four locations where we focus our eyes. This pattern teaches us when to make eye contact and when not to and describes the effects of both making and not making eye contact.

- Pattern 2, Transitions Between Points of Focus—provides us with the ability to seamlessly transition between these locations.

- Pattern 3, Peripheral Sight—explains an essential group dynamic skill. Most models of communication are designed for one-on-one communication. Simply put, we see where we look. This pattern teaches us how to see not only where we look but also where we are not looking which is critical for group communication.

To be respectful of gender equality and yet provide the reader with a fluid reading style, in this section the communicator is referred to by female pronouns and other people are referred to by male pronouns.

1-1

Pattern 1. Points of Focus

You may not even know this psychologist's name and yet your behavior stems from his teaching. You make more eye contact when communicating with people because of his modeling. You probably have never read his book, *On Becoming a Person* and yet you know the concept of empathy. Who is this man? Carl Rogers—the originator of "unconditional acceptance" of others.

Like most people, I was over trained in eye contact; in my case, I had the privilege of personal training with Carl Rogers. I was taught, and I believed that eye contact conveys caring and expresses sincerity. During the ten years following Carl Rogers' trainings, I practiced eye contact during all exchanges with others. And with 70-80% of the people I got amazing results because of this habit. I didn't understand why the other 20-30% were not receptive. Then after ten years of attentive listening with eye contact it struck me: Carl was in private practice so he never saw someone who didn't want to see him. The insight was that my 20-30% were the people who didn't want to see me but had to.

Points of Focus opens the 21 Pentimento Patterns. Even twenty years from now this skill will still be your favorite. You will finally understand under what conditions to make and hold eye contact and when not to. Welcome to the "in-sight" pattern.

There are directions for staging in theatre. The locations are given names (e.g., front right) so that quick reference can be made. So, too, in communication there are labels for the various locations toward which a communicator looks.

1

- **One-point**: looking down

- **Two-point**: looking at the other person; eye-contact

- **Three-point**: looking together at something close by, such as a paper

- **Four-point**: looking together at something farther away; looking across the room or outside the room.

One-point Communication

Looking down can signal several meanings. One interpretation is that the person has gone inside. This can be used to emphasize an emotion on a non-verbal level. "I am feeling [*looks down, simultaneous movement of the hand to the chest*] that we [*looks at the audience*]…" The non-verbal components transform the literal words into a powerful message.

Looking down at one-point can also be used to separate one piece of content from another one. Watch TV newscasters. Before starting a different news item they usually look down. They do not do this to look at their notes, since their text is presented to them on a prompter above the camera. Rather, they look down to signal the TV viewers that the present topic is closed and that a different news item is coming now.

The concept of looking down isn't restricted to newscasts. It is notable to mention the correlation between closing the eyes and looking down. When the individual looks up it is more likely that the eyes are open; yet eyes tend to close when looking down. Closing one's eyes and looking down increases one's ability to get in touch with one's feelings. Notice when you and others look down; this usually indicates that a transition to something "private" is occurring.

There is a direct correlation between visually-oriented people having an easier time dissociating from emotions and the kinesthetic-oriented population having an easier time associating with their feelings. When thinking, the visual-oriented people look up while the kinesthetic-oriented people tend to look down.

An example of looking down is a person praying. Prayer is usually a one-point communication during which the person is looking down although sometimes the individual will look up. It seems the more public (e.g., oral recitation) the prayer the more the person looks down.

Two-point Communication

In Western cultures people naturally make eye contact when talking. In some oriental cultures people avoid direct eye contact in certain situations. For instance, in a job interview in Japan the interviewee would never look at the face of the interviewer but rather at the knot of that person's necktie. Eye contact in such a situation would be considered as showing a lack of respect. However, when this same person later tells some friends how the interview went, eye contact among them will just be the same as it would be in the Western world.

In the Western world the more the content is positive, the better it is to have eye contact.

Three-point Communication

When the content is volatile it is recommended the communicator look at a third point. If the problem is represented on a flipchart or a piece of paper or symbolically represented by some object, it is quite natural to look at that third-point when mentioning the problem. Ideally, the communicator will stand or sit at an angle of 90 degrees to her listener. This will make it easy to switch from two-point to three-point.

Vignette: The Calculator

At the end of a two-week tour of presentations in Europe, my friend and sponsor, Rudolf, was finalizing the amount of honorarium. I was delightfully surprised when he handed me his calculator and said, "See if the calculator figured correctly." He had set a context of *us* checking *the calculator's* work. I laughed realizing that by using the third point of the machine and saying *the calculator* we would be fine if we needed to adjust the amount. The inanimate object circumvented any possible defensiveness.

> *Positive interactions* → *Two-Point*
> *Negative Interactions* → *Three-Point*

Deciding whether to use a two-point or a three-point style of communication begs the question of manipulation. The dictionary lists m*anipulation* as "skillful handling or operation, artful management or control." While the word manipulation often has a negative connotation, this book uses the term as defined by the dictionary with its favorable connotation of "artful." Especially in a conflict situation, skillful handling of the situation is helpful to all concerned. At those times, the communicator wants to know what works for others when she is interacting with them and at the same time, she wants people in her world to know what works for her.

This is not the same as trying to control the other person. As previously mentioned, if you think you can really *control* someone, just try to raise a teenager.

Vignette: Car Keys

When our children were adolescents, we openly shared with them what worked for us. With mom, the kids did well to look at her when explaining things. With me, if they were asking for the car keys or permission to do something unusual, it was more effective to touch me and study my face. If it looked like the answer was going to be "No," it was advisable to tap me on the shoulder and run out of the room shouting, "Think about it, Dad!" Everyone knew that once I said, "No," I was unlikely to change my response so they didn't want to let me give a definitive answer. Our children were not controlling us, but they were skillful in the way they adapted to our communication patterns.

Four-point Communication

When a communicator looks backwards over her shoulder or out of the window, she is referring to something that isn't immediately present. She is using a four-point communication. The fourth point is a point that has not yet been used as a reference point. It often symbolizes the past, the future, or people or things that are not present.

Pattern 2. Transitions Between Points of Focus

2

The first pattern was on when and when not to make eye contact. We learned the difference between two-point communication and three-point communication and that the message we wish to communicate influences not only our words but also our degree of eye contact. That is, we use two-point when the content is positive and three-point when the content deals with problems or less-than-positive content. Yet masterful communicators don't restrict themselves to deciding between either the two-point or three-point template—they switch between styles. This pattern teaches us how to maneuver between the two styles. Using these transitions correctly will hold our listeners' attention better.

Think of a university professor who looks only at her notes, never at the class or at a chalkboard or screen. That's an example of one-point communication. Pretty boring. Or imagine a college professor who draws diagrams on the board/overhead and never looks at the lecture hall students (strictly a third-point communication). Compare those professors with a more interesting lecturer, one who engages her audience with eye contact (two-point), displays visual information (three-point) and checks with her notes at the lectern (one-point).

Like the skilled lecturer, we too want to vary our points of focus. The transitions between the points not only maintain interest, but also greatly facilitate the listener's ability to follow. Although switching between points is natural for most of us, some refinements will make us even more effective. It's a matter of becoming more systematic, of knowing when and how to switch to keep our listener's attention. The most common points of focus that we switch between are the two and three-points. The skill used to switch from a three-point to a two-point is called "The Swing." The skill used to switch from a two-point to a three-point is called "Eye and Hand Coordination.

1-2

The Swing

The Transition from a Three-point to a Two-point

When the listener is looking at a piece of paper (a third point), the listener has the option of looking away from the paper to access his mental screen. This is where the listener pictures concepts, recalls memories, and envisions possibilities. However, when engaged in a two-point conversation, the listener often feels compelled to maintain eye contact with the speaker. The closer the speaker physically is to the listener the harder it is for the listener to access his mental screen. Why this is? A person has a mental screen that is about an arm's length distance from his face.

> *When the listener is looking at the third point, the listener has the choice of accessing his mental screen.*

Because of the listener's need to access his mental screen, it is important that the speaker swing away from the listener when making the transition from a three-point to the two-point format. The "swing" provides the listener with the appropriate mental picturing space, thus giving the listener a chance to reflect on the content.

As a learner

Least Recommended: Without the Swing

2

To test the importance of the listener having the needed distance to access his mental screen, do the following. Pair up with a partner. You are the speaker and your partner is the listener. Both of you are seated and looking at a piece of paper as you talk about the information on the paper. As both you and your partner are facing toward the piece of paper, notice how your elbows and heads are physically close to each other. As you intentionally stay physically close, turn to your partner, making eye contact, while saying, "Does that make sense?" By staying too close—*in his face*—you violate your partner's need for an arm's length space to access his mental screen.

Switch roles and perform the same experiment. Debrief the experience from both the perspective of being the speaker and the listener. The experience is often jarring for both parties. Statistically the eye contact at such close quarters is even more startling for the listener. Why does the listener feel more invaded by the speaker's close proximity than does the speaker? Often the speaker is sharing information that the speaker is more familiar with than is the listener. The speaker doesn't have the need to access her mental screen like the listener does.

Recommended: With the Swing

Repeat the experiment. Again both you and your partner are looking at the paper. This time you swing your torso away from your partner, making eye contact while saying, "Does that make sense?" Switch roles and perform the same maneuver. Debrief what the experience was like for both the speaker and the listener. Statistically both parties feel more comfortable with the swing than when the swing isn't used. The swing is both a movement of the speaker away from the listener when there is eye contact and a twisting of the torso toward the listener when both are looking at a third point.

Now try the swing standing. Pretend you are colleagues who were passing in the hallway and have stopped for a moment to talk about a third point—an agenda for next Tuesday's meeting. Notice how standing allows an even greater distance to swing.

Oral vs. Visual Communication

Two-point interactions are primarily oral communication and often are about the "relationship" level of parties. Three-point interactions add the visual component and often are about the "issue/content." Positive communication about issues works well with either two-point or three-point. However, if the interaction is about volatile information then a three-point visual interaction is definitely recommended. During such conversations the speaker will need to rotate between looking at the third point and looking at the listener (two-point).

> *If the interaction is about volatile information, do a three-point communication.*

When the third point is about volatile information the transition from a three-point to a two-point is the most important transition between all the points of focus. Why?

2

The communicator doesn't want to contaminate the relationship by bringing "issues" into the "relationship." ("How Not to Get Shot" which starts on page 174 will cover this in depth.) The communicator wants to disconnect the issues discussed at the third point from her relationship at the second point. This is what the Swing technique does.

The following axioms apply. If the content is positive then the communicator has the option of connecting the two-point (eye contact) with the third point. Hey, it never hurts to spill the positive over into the negative. She also has the option of preserving the "positive" at the second point by disconnecting or separating the second point from third point.

However, when the content at the third point is negative the communicator wants to avoid connecting this negativity back to the two-point eye contact.

Patterns 18 and 19 further explain the difference between connecting and disconnecting in transitions between second and third points.

Eye and Hand Coordination

1-3

The Transition from Two-point to Three-point

The listener consciously follows the speaker's eyes. So if the communicator wants a listener to look at something (a third point), she also looks at it rather than keeping her eyes on the listener's face. Why? Because if she gestures toward the third point but mistakenly keeps looking at her listener, the listener will likely continue to look right back at her instead of at the third point. This mistake is most likely to occur when the speaker is at a two-point and switches to a three-point. The transition from two-point to three-point is based on the principle, "the listener follows the speaker's eyes, not the speaker's hand gesture." The goal is to have "eye and hand coordination."

> *The listener follows our eyes, not our hands.*
> *So, point where we look and look where we point.*

As a learner

TV Weather Forecasters

The next time you are watching TV notice several weather forecasters. The meteorologists can look either at the map or at the camera. When they look the map notice how you, as a viewer, also look at the map. Yet when they point to the map but look at the camera notice how you look at them instead of at the map.

Vanna White (of the TV show *Wheel of Fortune)* has made a career in the art of "Eye and Hand Coordination." When she walks across the stage, her eyes are focused on the board. Her eyes follow her hand as she touches the lighted square. When she turns her head and makes eye contact with the audience, she signals that it is time for a question/spin.

1-4

Refinement: Credibility and Approachability

The speaker has two ways to point to a third-point location. One is by bouncing the hand to the location and the other is by holding the hand still (i.e., sideways) when pointing. When the speaker bounces her pointing hand, the listener views her as being approachable. The wrist is usually slightly bent and the fingers are usually curled. When the speaker holds her hand straight and still when pointing, the speaker conveys credibility. Pattern 4 will further explain the importance of Credibility and Approachability.

Refinement: Two-hand Gesturing

1-5

Often when the communicator is looking at the third point (e.g., a white board) with one hand pointing to it, she cannot see her listeners' reactions. By keeping the one hand pointing to the third point, she can turn and look directly at her listeners, thus getting a read on them while still indicating that she will return to the content of the third point. When she is ready, she can use the other hand to coordinate with her eye gaze as she non-verbally invites her listeners to look again at the third point. Bottom line: use one hand for content, the other hand for inviting people to look at the content.

Pattern 3. Peripheral Sight

1-6

When we reflect on "communication" the image that comes to mind is usually one-on-one communication. We so equate "communication" with person-to-person interaction that we think that communication in a group setting is just an extension of the one-on-one model. It isn't!

When we are talking to just one person we maintain eye contact. Literally we look where we see and see where we look. But in a group setting we can't possibly look at everyone at the same time yet we need to see how people are responding. We have to be able to see where we are not looking. Peripheral Sight is the skill most needed in order to make an effective transition from one-on-one communication to group communication.

Not surprisingly, this skill will also be valuable in one-on-one communication.

As communicators, we want to be able to read how the other person is receiving our message so we can adjust to their reactions. Why is it important to read the audience and adjust our communication? Because if listeners are rejecting our message, there is no point in continuing to do the same thing. Reading the listener is fairly easy when we can look directly at our listeners. Sometimes, however, listeners do not want us to look at them directly. There are various possible reasons for this. Maybe the listener is shy. Maybe he is culturally deferring by not looking at us. Or it may even be that he is withdrawing as a way to passively influence us. Whatever the reason, it is important for us to be able to see listeners' reactions "out of the corner of our eye" while we continue looking at a first, third or fourth point.

As a learner

Training Your Peripheral Perception

There are many ways to train your peripheral perception. One way is to turn yourself 45 degrees away from a TV, look at a point in front of you and watch the changes on the TV screen. Some of us when we were kids would hold both of our hands at arms length in front of our faces. Then, wiggling our index fingers, we would gradually move both hands out to the side until they were in line with our shoulders. We tried to see the wiggling index fingers even when the hands were past our ears. Survival instincts foster peripheral viewing. The human range of seeing movement is about 180°, dogs can see around 240° and cats can see even further. The next time you walk into someone's presence, notice how the individual registers (e.g., blinks) an awareness of you at about 180°.

3

Vignette: Hunters

When two people are deer hunting (for the sake of identification we will presume one hunter is a female and the other is male), they are standing side by side, each looking straight ahead. If a deer moves directly in front of the male hunter, the female will often shoot before the man. Why? The human eyes are designed to see movement when the movement occurs at a 45° angle from where the eyes are looking. The function of having two eyes in the front of the head is to provide depth perception. That's why the female who was seeing from a 45° angle was able to perceive the deer's movement a split second before the male (who was looking straight at the deer) could notice the movement.

In the Western European cultures, eye contact is often seen as positive. It conveys "caring/attention." It is equated with integrity. In school when a teacher is in the hallway disciplining a disruptive student, the educator is known to say, "Look at me when I am talking to you." In reality, though, eye contact is not intrinsically positive or negative.

Vignette: Tourists and Street Vendors

Our first two days spent in a fine resort city were a shock to Gail and me. As the street vendors approached us with their big, beautiful brown eyes, we knew we didn't need another sombrero yet we wanted to be respectfully polite when refusing. Initially when we were approached, we would stop walking and make full facial contact as we said, "No." We soon realized that stopping only resulted in more vendors approaching us. It still feels less than humane not to make eye contact or even to say, "No" as we pass the vendors. Yet the experience demonstrates two things: first, the non-verbal level of communication is more important than the verbal level and second, one cannot ethnocentrically interpret another culture's non-verbals. While I might feel like I am brushing them off, I am actually communicating much more clearly than stopping and explaining why I am not purchasing their product.

Vignette: Managers

When a referee separates two professional fighters, he does so by pushing the combatants apart with no eye contact. To do otherwise is to show partiality. The most dangerous call for the police to respond to is domestic violence. The officers are trained to separate the parties by standing at the person's side, nodding their heads and without eye contact gently guiding the people into separate rooms. Both the referee and the officer are employing the same skill—peripheral sight. For their own safety, they must be able to see the people at all times and still not become engaged.

3

> The two variables that cause engagement and, in many cases, escalation are being verbal and making eye contact.

Not just tourists and managers have to rethink whether to automatically make eye contact. This extends to classroom teachers and parents as well. If the child is inappropriate, the adult first gets his attention (usually by being verbal and looking at him). Then, as the child starts to look up, the adult breaks eye contact and slowly does a non-verbal signal to indicate the appropriate behavior. Truthfully, the child has memorized all our sermonettes—there is no need for the parent or teacher to talk.

All these managers, referees, officers, parents and teachers all have one thing in common—they want to gain compliance and at the same time preserve the relationship. It starts with *Peripheral Sight*. In a real sense, the goal is to manage the individual's *behavior* not their person.

When managing someone, we may initially need to be verbal and make eye contact. As soon as we have the person's attention, stop eye contact, being verbal and switch to non-verbal signals. This preserves the relationship.

Manage the individual's behavior not their person.

Notes

Chapter Two

Auditory Patterns

Overview

What we say is the verbal level of communication. How we say the verbiage is non-verbal communication. Think about how you say, "I love you" to your parent, and compare it with how you would say the same thing to your spouse on your wedding day. Auditory non-verbal communication pertains to how we use our voice. There are three patterns.

- Pattern 4, Voice Patterns: Credibility and Approachability—delineates the differences between the two most-used voice patterns. This pattern clarifies how our voice conveys whether we are sending or seeking information.

- Pattern 5, Voice Speed and Volume—explains the importance and impact of our voice speed and volume. This understanding will be the basis for Pattern 17: Influencing Another's Breathing, which is the most sophisticated Pentimento Pattern.

- Pattern 6, ABOVE (Pause) Whisper—presents one of the most important group dynamic patterns. This pattern details how to get a group's attention. The ABOVE startles the group. The *Pause* (done with the frozen hand gesture) picks up the stragglers and allows the group to catch their breath. Then the *Whisper* lets the group lower their metabolism.

To be respectful of gender equality and yet provide the reader with a fluid reading style, in this section the communicator is referred to by male pronouns and other people are referred to by female pronouns.

1-7~16

Pattern 4. Voice Patterns: Credibility and Approachability

The more a culture is industrialized and educated the more the visual form of communicating increases and is preferred. However, there is a paradox: the more visual a society is, the more easily it can be influenced by a communicator who is skilled in the auditory style because the listeners in an industrial society are less skilled in the auditory style. Therefore, by taking time to learn and practice effective voice patterns, a communicator will increase his ability to influence even the most sophisticated listeners.

Effective oral communication includes both talking and pausing; it's a series of "content" (spoken), pause, "content" (spoken), and pause. First, let's consider the spoken part. The all-important Pause will be covered in Pattern 9 and Pattern 18.

Even though the listener may not be aware of the communicator's voice patterns, she is greatly affected by the communicator's intonation and how flat or rhythmic his voice is. These voice patterns can be placed on a continuum. A voice pattern that is flat and that drops on the last accentuated syllable before the end of the sentence or before a pause (falling intonation) is perceived as credible. The credible voice pattern is used when sending information, to stress the importance of the message, or to give it more emphasis. In contrast, a voice with a rolling intonation that curls up on the last accentuated syllable before the end of the sentence or before a pause is perceived as approachable. The approachable voice pattern is used when seeking information, to emphasize relationship, or to soften the emphasis.

> *Credible voice—sends information*
> *Approachable voice—seeks information*

Three Phases of Conversation

1-17

4

The three phases of a conversation are: speaking, listening and pausing. At a first glance it may sound unusual, but the voice patterns of credibility and approachability manifest themselves not only when someone is speaking but also as the speaker listens and pauses.

	Credibility	**Approachability**
Speaking		
head	still	bobs
voice	flat ———	rhythmic
intonations	curls down	curls up
style	soliloquy	includes others
Listening		
sits	straight	leans forward
head	still	bobs
silence/sounds	is silent	makes encouraging sounds
if talks	interrupts	says name and asks questions
Pausing	Has an easier time remaining silent. Occasionally needs to breathe deeper for listener's perception that speaker is OK.	Has a hard time remaining silent. Tends to have no pause because of fear of losing listener's attentiveness.

Refinement: Gender Communication

1-18

The voice patterns have a high correlation with several other concepts. For example, John Gray (*Men are From Mars, Women are from Venus*) and Deborah Tannen (notably *You Just Don't Understand*)[6] have pointed out that traditionally the male voice pattern is considered more akin to credibility and the female voice pattern is seen more toward the approachability end of the voice pattern continuum.

Deborah Tannen and John Gray have increased the public's awareness of the fact that genders communicate differently to the point that their styles could be considered "cultures." With so much written on the subject, this work will devote only a short section to how the cultures interact with each other when negotiating and managing. What follows are stereotypes; hopefully, the reader will be insulted by them, which is a good sign of how our larger society is changing for the better.

Category	Masculine/ Credible *when listening*	Feminine/ Approachable *when listening*
head	still	nods
sounds	silence	makes encouraging sounds
posture	sits back	leans forward
touch	none	could be
pressure	onus is on other	helping/assisting
style	competitive	cooperative
oriented	individuals	team

A listener's style influences how the speaker interprets the listener's style. The three listening styles are: a style associated with the listener's gender, the style associated with the opposite gender, or a blend of both styles.

When the subordinate is a male, he tends to interpret the male boss, who is listening in the statistically male manner, in the same way that the male boss intended; namely, he assumes that the male boss is silently processing the information. But when the male subordinate is talking to a female boss who is listening in the statistically female style, the male subordinate is likely to infer the female boss is in agreement with the subordinate's idea, whereas the female boss was meaning to indicate she supports the male subordinate as a person, encouraging him to bring his ideas and input to her.

When a female subordinate is talking to a female boss who is listening in the statistically female style, the subordinate interprets the boss as the boss had hoped; the subordinate believes the boss is supportive of the conversation. But when the female subordinate is conversing with a male boss who is listening in the traditionally-male credible style, the female subordinate might infer that the male boss is not caring or following the conversation closely enough.

The following chart summarizes the statistical ways that the subordinate interprets the boss. The subordinate wants to notice how the top four lines of the chart are common interpretations. The bottom four lines are still becoming more common. The subordinate wants to be aware of his or her innate reactions and stay open to the possibility that, as a communicator, the subordinate needs to calibrate to what each boss' style is and know how to accurately interpret what the boss' intentions might be.

Subordinate's Gender	Boss' Gender	Boss' Style	Subordinate's Interpretation of Boss
male	male	male	= processing the info
female	female	female	= following the info
male	female	female	= "She could be agreeing, and yet I could be mistaken."
female	male	male	= "He may not be agreeing or following, and yet I could be mistaken."
male	male	female	= wimp, pushover
female	female	male	= offended, abandoned
male	female	male	= cold, sterile
female	male	female	= sensitive, new-age guy

Refinement: Compliments

An interesting side note to "gender misinterpretation" is the concept of compliments. When a boss gives a compliment to a subordinate, it can be done with the credible voice pattern or the approachable voice pattern. If the compliment is given with a credible voice, then the subordinate is receiving the praise from the boss' *position* and not from the boss *personally*. On the other hand, if the compliment is given with an approachable voice, then the subordinate feels the praise is coming from the boss as a *person*. The following are axioms regarding compliments and voice patterns:

• Initially male and female subordinates can be motivated by compliments from the boss' *position*.

- The longer the subordinate works for a boss the more the subordinate is motivated more by the boss' *person* giving the compliment.

- Compared to the male, the female subordinate is likely to be motivated sooner by compliments from the boss' *person*.

4

Year	Boss' Gender		Boss' Voice	Subordinate's Response (Male)
1	m		credible	very motivating
1		f	credible	likes compliment and boss genderless
1	m		approachable	likes compliment and confused by boss' voice
1		f	approachable	expects and likes boss' femininity and yet would rather get a credible voice compliment; finds it confusing
2	m		credible	somewhat likes compliment; is motivated by it
2		f	credible	used to what he calls a sterile boss and is not motivated by compliment
2	m		approachable	very motivated by the personalness of boss
2		f	approachable	very motivated by the platonic relationship with boss

Year	Boss' Gender		Boss' Voice	Subordinate's Response (Female)
1	m		credible	somewhat likes compliment but confused by it; "Why did he use that voice?"
1		f	credible	emotionally abandoned
1	m		approachable	delightfully surprised and motivated
1		f	approachable	was hoping it would be like this and is motivated.
2	m		credible	} used to "spock." not motivated;
2		f	credible	} let's find a head hunter.
2	m		approachable	} I am so satisfied working here
2		f	approachable	}

A corollary to compliments is a boss' apology for having a bad day. In most organizations it is likely to be acceptable for the boss' *person* to have a bad day, but the boss' *position* is not allowed to have a bad day. The *position* is expected to perform well at all times. Later, if an apology is offered, it is best to have it come from the *person* (done vulnerably). A sincere apology from a boss' *person* will often increase the subordinate's admiration for his boss.

Refinement: Position(al) Communication

Of special importance is the way in which voice patterns correlate with positions inside an organization. The lower position person tends to speak in an approachable voice pattern when interacting, especially with superiors. The person with an approachable voice pattern is seen as seeking information and open to suggestions. In contrast, the higher position person tends to speak in a credible voice. The person with a credible voice pattern is seen as sending a message and less open to receiving new information.

If someone were blindfolded and walked around the floors of an organization's building, he could figure out what level of leadership worked on each floor by listening to the voices of the personnel working on each particular floor. The lower floors typically have the lower positions. The voice patterns on these floors are rhythmic and end with an intonation that tends to curl up. Voice patterns are different on the higher floors. On the upper floors the voices are flatter and more guttural indicating the presence of executives. Hey, they like the view from the higher elevation. Inadvertently, upper management's voice patterns convey that they are not receptive to feedback. It explains the oft-heard complaint of subordinates, "My boss doesn't really know or care what's going on in the company."

The symbolism of different floors representing layers of an organization can be extended to several patterns of communication:

4

- Tension easily flows downhill. And like a snowball picks up size the farther downhill it rolls, tension increases as it moves from upper to lower levels.

- Information, like water, needs help to go uphill. The higher the administrator is the more he doesn't have accurate information about what is really occurring.

- A middle level manager is highly valued if she can carry information to uninformed bosses and not shock the bosses too much.

- The inability of organizations to create Learning Communities (see Peter Senge's work[7]) can be traced to the voice patterns of the upper echelons of an organization. Literally, the higher one is promoted the more the person is supposed to *know* instead of supposed to *learn*. Learning Communities and egalitarian structures cannot be created until the voice patterns associated with authority are addressed. Organizations need to teach people in their upper and middle echelons to use an approachable voice pattern when seeking information and input. It will ensure that management is better informed about what is going on in the lower echelons, thus avoiding the unpleasant surprises that occur when upper levels are out of touch with reality. Another benefit of knowing when and how to use the approachable voice is that it helps managers create the genuine Learning Communities that Peter

Senge speaks of. And as referenced in the previous "Compliment Chart," having an organization that systematically uses both the credible and approachable voices patterns increases the employees' job satisfaction and decreases the bills from head hunters.

- When a lower position feels pressure/tension from a high position the lower position will withhold information. This withholding of information, sometimes called passive aggressiveness, can occur without either position being aware that it is happening.

Refinement: Decision-making Process

Why do some people get promoted while others of equal ability do not? People who get things done with ease are promoted and given more challenges. The ease of getting things done is often based on one's effective navigation with the decision-making process. A person's voice greatly influences how one successfully handles this process. Having a wide range of voices and knowing when to systematically use them can be the key to upward mobility.

In the previous 'refinement' the correlation between voice patterns and positions was presented. That is, the higher position individual will tend to use a credible voice pattern when communicating with a subordinate and the subordinate will tend to use an approachable voice pattern when talking to a superior. When participants with equal status make decisions, the two voice patterns influence the process. Listeners interpret the credible voice as sending information, as requiring that they accept the information without question. In contrast, listeners interpret the approachable voice as seeking information, as inviting them to share their own information and viewpoints.

Statistically, the individual with the most credible voice pattern will tend to have the most influence on the outcome. Simply put, among equals, the person with the more credible voice pattern is seen as having a higher position.

Each voice pattern is valued differently based on what phase of the decision-making process is involved. The decision-making process is made up of four phases:

Gathering	Evaluating	Deciding	Implementing

During the Gathering phase the more pertinent information found, the better. The *approachable* voice pattern is welcomed because such a voice pattern elicits more information. As previously mentioned the approachable voice pattern, associated with females, tends to elicit more information. That's why the flow of information is greater if females are facilitating.[8]

The word "decide" comes from the Latin word "to cut." During the Deciding phase the purpose is to reduce or cut the options gathered. During this phase the *credible* voice, associated with males, tends to exude the definitiveness that is often held in esteem by busy people, by those who like to "cut to the chase." That's why decisions are reached more quickly if males are facilitating.

Is the social correlation between the male being credible and the female being approachable irreversible?

Not at all. In fact, the modern male is allowed, and even at times encouraged, to switch from the credible sending-information pattern to the approachable seeking-information pattern. Such switching actually adds to their gender appeal. These are "Sensitive, New-Age-Guys." Unfortunately, our society still has few positive descriptions for the female who switches from the approachable seeking-information pattern to the credible sending-information pattern.

Culture

The focus so far has been on individuals within the group. Understanding how the group as a whole operates is also useful. Most models of communication are one-on-one models. As previously mentioned, the tendency is to think that group communication is an extension of one-on-one communication. It is not. A group is more than a composite of its individual members. It is an entity in and of itself. When a group has operated as a unit for a while a group culture develops. Cultures can be described as mostly credible, mostly approachable, or a mixture of credible and approachable. These three cultures have predictable ways of operating.

In the credible culture (or in a mixed culture that overemphasizes the *credible* voices), the group is quick to leave the Gathering phase and quick to arrive at a decision. Whether the credible culture has gathered the appropriate information is always questionable. The more the committee is composed of high-level positions (e.g., district office personnel), the more this pattern occurs. For credible cultures, saving time is often more important than the validity of the decision.

Gathering	**Evaluating**	**Deciding**	Implementing
credible-oriented people			

In an approachable culture (or in a mixed culture that over-emphasizes the approachable voices), the Gathering phase lasts longer and more information is obtained. In fact, the group is reluctant to leave the Gathering phase. When it comes to making a decision, they tend to procrastinate for fear that the decision might offend or impose upon individuals. If they think of one person who might be adversely affected by a decision they will procrastinate. They seek consensus and harmony.

Gathering	Evaluating	Deciding	Implementing
approachable -oriented people			

No Monopoly

Neither approachable people nor credible people have a monopoly on making good decisions. The title "implementing" is faded to illustrate this point. The approachable people don't necessarily make good decisions because they are reluctant to decide. And then when approachable people finally do make a decision they are sometimes so embarrassed about what they decided that they won't pay attention to results during the implementation phase. The credible people don't necessarily make good decisions because they are so busy that they often don't take the time to gather the necessary information in order to make a decision. And then when the credible people have made a decision they are so busy with the next set of decisions they are making they don't have time to check on how the last set of decisions was carried out.

As Peter Senge says, we don't know the effect of our actions.[9] That is because we are either too embarrassed to know what actually was implemented or are too busy to track what was implemented.

In healthy groups where both credibility and approachability are valued, approachability is sought during the Gathering phase and credibility during the Evaluating and especially the Deciding phases. The chart below uses a wavy line that curls up at the end to represent approachable-oriented people. The chart uses a straight line that curls down at the end to represent credible-oriented people.

Gathering	Evaluating	Deciding	Implementing
valued	*valued*	*valued*	

Refinement: Intervention Speed Based on Culture

There are times when an individual is not productive enough and needs to be managed in order to preserve the functionality of the group. The wisdom of whether to manage immediately or to wait is best determined by understanding the culture of the group.

The more the person-in-charge recognizes his own innate management style, the more he can adjust to the culture of the group. Credible-oriented people intervene quickly and manage swiftly. Approachable-oriented people intervene slowly and manage reluctantly. A credible-oriented person-in-charge can be himself and manage early when dealing with a credible-oriented group but must increase his patience when managing an approachable-oriented group. When working with the credible-oriented group, the approachable person-in-charge needs to increase the speed with which he intervenes.

The following graphic shows the four combinations possible when the management of an inappropriate individual occurs. Because of the complexity of group dynamics, a triangle icon is used to show that pressure felt on one side is equally experienced by the other two sides. The corners are represented by P (person-in-charge), I (individual) and G (the group as a whole).

The flat arrow with the intonation curling down symbolizes the credible voice/culture. The rolling arrow with an intonation curling up is the icon for the approachable voice/culture. In the top row of the graphic the groups are credible. In the bottom row, the groups are approachable. In the left column, the person-in-charge is credible. In the right column, the person-in-charge is approachable.

Credible Culture

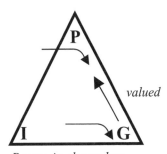

valued

Person-in-charge has excellent timing.

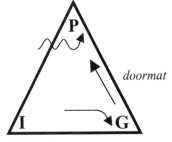

doormat

Person-in-charge seen as "soft;" needs to intervene sooner.

Approachable Culture

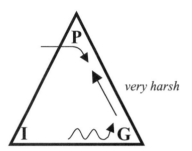

very harsh

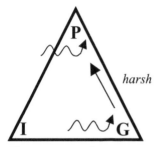

harsh

The person-in-charge is seen as harsh; needs to be patient. Person-in-charge won't be bothered by the group criticizing him.

The person-in-charge is naturally patient, and when he finally intervenes, he is bothered by the group's private criticism of him.

Credible-oriented people-in-charge want to increase their awareness of the individuals.

Approachable-oriented people-in-charge want to notice the people as a whole group.

People-in-charge of both styles have to understand the ambivalence that an approachable-oriented group will have when the person-in-charge manages an inappropriate individual. An approachable-oriented group will outwardly say that the person-in-charge's management of the individual was too harsh. And yet each member will inwardly likely appreciate that the intervention was done. The approachable person-in-charge is bothered by the group seeing him as harsh. The credible person-in-charge isn't bothered. After managing the individual, the approachable person-in-charge often apologizes to the group which confuses the group. It is dangerous to manage from your approachable persona.

It seems strange that the approachable member inwardly appreciates that the person-in-charge intervened but publicly won't indicate such appreciation. The following research explains this phenomenon.

Friesen and Ekman[10] did an experiment in which the facial expressions of American and Japanese people were covertly videotaped as they watched a horrific film of an industrial accident. Because the Japanese culture places a higher value on masking one's emotions, the researchers expected to see less emotional reaction from the Japanese participants. They were not disappointed. When the Japanese saw the footage together, they were stoic. And, in fact, when an official-looking, white-coated researcher stayed in the room with individual Japanese participants, each participant still was stoic. The American participants showed a wide range of distressed facial expressions.

When an individual from either culture thought no one was watching (i.e., no white-coated researcher was present), the individuals of both cultures showed similarly distressed facial expressions. This led Friesen and Ekman to conclude that even when a culture has strict rules about public displays of emotion, its people still use the same basic facial expressions in private.

Refinement: Three Levels of Communication

Credible-oriented people tend to see people as a means to an end. Subordinates are held accountable in a fair and equitable manner. The group is more important than the individual member. Approachable-oriented people are exactly the opposite; they tend to see that the individual is to be honored at all costs. In this regard, the differences between credible-oriented and approachable-oriented people can be overlaid on Fisher and Ury's model of three levels of communication.[11]

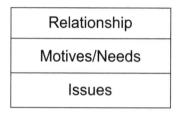

Credible individuals focus on the issue level and have to be taught to be attentive to the people involved (relationship). Approachable individuals focus on the relationship level and have to be coached to expand their focus to include the issues involved.

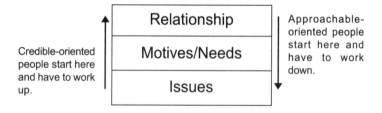

Whether the focus is on the relationship or on the issues, both styles are appropriate for certain contexts. The military, out of necessity, functions from the premise that the good of the whole outweighs the needs of the few. Gandhi also operated from this premise. The world of counselors is exactly the opposite. The unit (e.g., family) can only function when each individual member is healthy.

Correlations Chart		
(Page)	**Credibility**	**Approachability**
Functions (p47)	sending info	seeking info
Gender (p47)	associated with males	associated with females
Compliments (p50)	positional	personal
Position (p52)	higher position	lower position
Positional (p52) **Decision-making**	hierarchical	egalitarian
Process (p54)	deciding	gathering
Management **Style** (p58)	intervenes quickly	intervenes slowly
Focus On (p61)	issues	relationships

4

Hybrid Voice Patterns

Few people have a voice pattern that is 100% credible or 100% approachable. Instead, people usually have a hybrid or a combination of the two voice patterns. Traditionally females are raised to use an approachable voice and males the credible voice pattern. When a person uses the voice pattern associated with the opposite gender the likelihood of the voice pattern being a hybrid increases. For instance, when males are asked to demonstrate a credible voice pattern or females to demonstrate the approachable voice pattern they can do it with ease. And when males and females are asked to demonstrate the opposite voice patterns, they usually can do so—almost. Males will typically attempt the approachable pattern by rolling their voices up and down as they begin a sentence, but when they reach the end of a phrase or sentence they tend to revert to the credible pattern in which the voice falls to a lower pitch. Likewise, females will keep their voices flat and credible until they come to the end of the phrase or sentence, but then their intonation tends to curl up.

1-19

Pattern 5. Voice Speed and Volume

In the play/movie, *My Fair Lady,* one professor bets another professor that he can pass off a street corner flower-selling female as a member of high society. We are all familiar with the many exercises that the professor put his student through—"The rain in Spain …" The show illustrates how much we are all affected by a person's voice patterns.

While Credibility and Approachability are the two main voice patterns, there are at least two other voice variables. To be an effective communicator we want to master all four variables.

The third and fourth variables in voice patterns are the elements of *speed* and *volume*. When the communicator's voice pattern is fast and loud, the listener's metabolism increases. When the communicator's voice pattern is slow and soft the listener's metabolism decreases. These variables are the basis for several of the Pentimento Patterns, notably Pattern 6 ABOVE (Pause) Whisper and Pattern 17 Influencing Another's Breathing.

Speed

When a communicator speaks faster than the listener is able to process the ideas, he increases his listener's metabolism. Likewise, when he speaks more slowly than the listener is used to and has her permission to do so, he lowers her metabolism. I went to college on the West coast and I had a hard time keeping up with the professors while I was taking notes. I was so relieved when we had a visiting professor from Texas who spoke with a slower speed than my other professors. The Texan certainly had my permission to talk that slowly... I was very calm during the lecture. Yet I had classmates who could take notes much faster than myself—they were frustrated with the speed of the guest professor and because not enough content was being covered, their metabolism went up.

Volume

There are times when a LOUD voice is needed. Often a presenter needs to use a LOUD voice to get a group's attention (for example, following lunch or during transitions from small group work back to focusing on the presenter). Another time when a LOUD voice might be needed is at a staff meeting when someone is outraged by a decision that the group is about to make. Member X pounds the table and yells, "No way! We need to focus on ..." More about the use of the LOUD voice in the next Pattern.

Long Term Memory

Every communicator has his baseline of behaviors. This is the person's normal range of visual patterns (facial expressions, points of focus), auditory patterns (credible and approachable, speed and volume), kinesthetic patterns (gestures, proximity to people, body posture) and breathing patterns (shallow and abdominal).

Normal baseline behavior range: VAKB

Whenever the communicator wants to "mark off" something important for the listener, he communicates outside his normal behavioral range. This creates long-term memory. He can either speak above (louder and faster) or below (softer and slower) his normal baseline volume. This axiom about the non-verbal components of voice speed and volume applies to all of our non-verbal signals. The brain is more attentive to that which is unique compared to that which is familiar. When the communicator's amplitude is outside his normal range, the listener's brain registers, "Oh! this is different. I need to remember this."

Amplitude above normal range

Normal baseline behavior range

Amplitude below the normal range

When the communicator increases his volume and speed, his listeners will recognize, based on his vehemence, that what he is saying is important to him. Is there any advantage to marking off below, instead of above, the one's normal range? Yes. When a communicator marks off with a whisper, the listener not only knows that he feels the message is important, the listener can also breathe better. The masters of the whisper are actors. Watch a video of one of Sidney Poitier's old movies and be mesmerized.

Communicators who exhibit a wide range of behaviors have others' permission to do a wider range of behaviors. Whatever the communicator's range of behavior, he should be systematic both inside and outside his normal range. An effective communicator doesn't use a range of behaviors randomly but intentionally selects a unique set of behaviors to increase the listener's long-term memory.

Pattern 6. ABOVE (Pause) Whisper

1-20~22

We have all experienced the lonely feeling of being responsible as the chair or presenter for getting things done
and yet we are having difficulty just getting the group's
attention. At the same time, we want to be both friendly
and productive. How do we get a group's attention in such
a way that we can do both? We do it by combining the
previous skills of Patterns 4 (credible and approachable)
and 5 (speed and volume).

6

This pattern helps us get the attention of a noisy group
quickly while keeping rapport and productivity high. It
involves using a high volume (ABOVE) followed by a
Pause, then a slow speed and low volume (Whisper). The
"ABOVE" is a blend of the credible tonality, high volume and fast speed. And the "Whisper" is a mixture of
the approachable tonality, low volume and slow speed.
CREDIBLE, LOUD, and FAST—pause—*approachable,
s o f t and s l o w.*

No matter how large or small the group, the ABOVE (Pause)
Whisper pattern is an ideal, never-fail technique for getting their attention. The speaker uses the *ABOVE* to shock
and interrupt the group. The group immediately becomes
quiet. The listeners' metabolism increases. The "Pause,"
especially when done with a Pattern 9 Frozen Hand Gesture, holds their attention. The Whisper lowers the listeners' metabolism, thus calming the group and allowing them
to hear the speaker's message.

Vignette: Good Will Hunting (a movie)

The influence of a *Whisper* is evidenced in an emotional scene from the movie, *Good Will Hunting*. Robin Williams is a psychologist who has been working with a young man, Will, who is a mathematical genius. Robin has been trying to release the shackles from the man's childhood that are holding him back from accomplishing all he can. In this climactic encounter, the patient finally stops resisting and starts to trust by lowering the drawbridge to his heart—he lets Williams in. Standing across from his client and friend, the counselor makes a quiet yet intense statement, "It's not your fault." The stored ache and agony of guilt and suppression explodes. It initially flows out as an angry volcano—Will physically wants to beat his counselor. But Robin keeps repeating in a whisper the emotional chorus of, "It's not your fault." The whisper allows the message to be heard as the man's anger melts to tears and he releases his pent-up emotions.

1-23

Refinement: Decontamination

Often the communicator has to be loud when doing the ABOVE to get the listeners' attention. By pausing [*usually done with a Frozen Hand Gesture* (Pattern 9)], while shifting to a new location [*doing a Break and Breathe* (Pattern 18)], and then starting the message in a Whisper, the communicator helps listeners separate the "traffic cop" persona who demanded their attention from the kind/gentle persona who whispered the message. This process of separating the bad guy from the good guy is called Decontamination (Pattern 8).

Drop your voice to a whisper, start the message, then gradually return to your normal speaking volume.

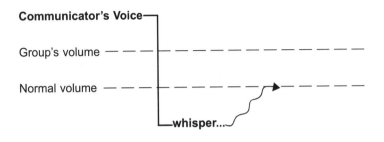

1-24

Refinement: Step-down

However, sometimes some of the audience hears and responds to the ABOVE while the rest of the group is not quieting down. From a group dynamic standpoint, the speaker cannot afford to wait (that is, pause long enough for the noisy ones to comply.) Therefore the speaker gradually lowers his voice, moving from the loud volume of the ABOVE down to the very soft volume of the Whisper. The speaker uses a softer and softer voice with each phrase. This Step-down Technique is designed to pick up the stragglers and to lower the metabolism of everyone.

Step down your voice to a whisper, start the message, then gradually return to your normal speaking volume.

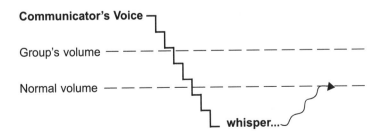

Refinement: Incomplete Sentence

The Incomplete Sentence, like the Step-down, is a variation of the ABOVE (Pause) Whisper. There are occasions when the group is restless (for example, the day before a long vacation or when there is dramatic change in the weather); at those times, the speaker/chair may have to be a "traffic cop." The speaker knows he will wear out his welcome with "LISTEN UP," "WAIT A MINUTE," "FOLKS, WE HAVE A LOT TO COVER." So, the speaker disguises the ABOVE by saying only the first two or three syllables of the message (for example, "RETURN-ING ...") with a perfectly still body; he then pauses in a one-point posture [*looking down*] (see page 29). As the group suddenly gets quiet, the speaker then moves to a different body position or location. In other words, the speaker *decontaminates* (see page 76) so the "traffic cop" won't interfere with the message. This is especially effective if the break is at an unnatural point (for example, "RETUR...ning to the next point").

Following the ABOVE, remember to pause, breathe, and then start the message in a whisper.

Chapter Three

Kinesthetic Patterns 【K】

Overview

Kinesthetic non-verbal communication is what we do with our body. The Kinesthetic category has the most patterns—eight:

- Pattern 7, Physical Presence—explains how our proximity and touch can be viewed as welcoming and comforting or unwelcome and threatening.

- Pattern 8, Decontamination—details how different locations can be used to assist communication. Decontamination is the favorite stress management pattern.

- Pattern 9, Frozen Hand Gesture—teaches us how to maintain a listener's attention while we pause in our speaking. Frozen Hand Gesture is the basis for more of the Pentimento Patterns than any other pattern. This pattern is the starting point for mastering non-verbal communication.

- Pattern 10, Gesturing: Four Quadrants—outlines the four directions toward which we can gesture. Gesturing to four different quadrants parallels what we learned in Pattern 1 which was the four locations toward which we can look.

To be respectful of gender equality and yet provide the reader with a fluid reading style, in this section the communicator is referred to by female pronouns and other people are referred to by male pronouns.

- Pattern 11, Gesturing: Assigning Attributes—delineates how our gestures can increase or decrease the energy and enthusiasm of our listeners.

- Pattern 12, Gestures of Relationship—provides us with a method for bonding people together.

- Pattern 13, High Expectations—enlightens us as to how we convey intelligence and expectations even when we are not talking. High Expectations lets us empower others by how we posture ourselves when we are silent.

- Pattern 14, Kinesthetic Equivalents of Credibility and Approachability—is the kissing cousin of Pattern 4, Voice Patterns: Credibility and Approachability. Pattern 4 taught us how powerful our voice patterns are. Pattern 14 allows us to be more congruent by coordinating our voice and body patterns.

Pattern 7. Physical Presence

1-26

The electronic age has changed our culture forever. The advice[12] that emerged at the beginning of this age still holds true "'High tech' needs high touch." We have all experienced the frustration of being put on hold by an electronic switchboard. We need more humanness. Touch provides human contact in an industrialized and educated world. Yet we daily read of sexual harassment lawsuits involving inappropriate touch so it is imperative to understand the impact that touch has. While there is prudence in adopting a policy of *no contact in the work place*, we also miss the wisdom of appropriate touch. This pattern will explain the impact of physical presence and also provide guidelines on how to use proximity and touch appropriately.

"Physical Presence" refers to touch and proximity. Touch and, to a lesser extent, proximity can greatly affect the communicator's and other person's metabolism. When a person's metabolism increases the person's breathing also quickens. (For more on the impact of metabolism in communication, see Breathing Patterns 15 - 17.) The brain receives less oxygen. With the brain not receiving its needed oxygen, the person reverts to emotional knee-jerk reactions. The likelihood of the interaction going well is decreased. Simply, metabolism and breathing are interconnected. When we keep our metabolism and others' metabolism lower, we increase our permission level (see page 4). Patterns 15 through 19 will cover in detail how to do this.

As a learner

Touch and Points of Focus

> Do this in pairs. Pretend you are in an office setting. Walk up to your partner who is seated at a desk. As you look at a third point (e.g., a paper in front of your partner) lightly touch your partner's shoulder and say, "How is the report coming along?"

> Approach a second time. This time wrap your face around in front of your seated partner. Hold this two-point eye contact while saying, "How is the report coming along?"

Most people breathe abdominally/lower when they are touched without eye contact. That is, they breathe better when the communicator is looking at a third point. Of course the relationship between the people has the greatest influence on how a touch is interpreted. Appropriate touch that is welcomed increases the positive relationship, so it is the relationship (and obviously, the context) that determines if the touch is appropriate. The medical community has a parallel. Often a doctor examines a patient's private parts. When this is done without eye contact, the patient interprets the doctor's look and touch as appropriate.

There are many ways that the communicator can influence a person's metabolism through touch. Depending on the type of touch (and proximity) the communicator can greatly affect the other person's breathing. One of the many by-products of an increased metabolism by the other person is that the individual becomes more attentive. Just like the "LOUD" caused an increase in listeners' metabolism so too can physical presence increase the other person's metabolism.

When a communicator is delivering a report to someone who is sitting at his desk, the communicator has a choice of laying the report on the desk or actually handing the report to him. Handing a report, sheet of paper, or an object to a person is an indirect form of touch. If there is a lingering Platonic moment when both parties are holding the report the communicator's physical presence is increased.

Vignette Ken and Kim

On their wedding day Ken and Kim made some promises to one another that weren't done at the altar. One of their pledges was to find a company that allowed them to work at the same place. They were overjoyed when *Visual Vision*, a medium size "events company," hired them. Their dream of traveling together to set up the company's events was finally realized.

Since they started at the same time they enjoyed sharing their evolving impressions of the company's culture with one another. Quickly they realized that they were much more kinesthetic than the other employees. They stood closer to people than others did. They naturally reached out to people and touched them. Ken shared that he tended to touch shoulders and Kim tended to touch forearms. They also noticed that Kim had more permission than Ken had.

They both realized that it was safer not to touch anyone in the workplace. However, when they were out of the office and on the road setting up the A-V equipment for a convention, they discovered exactly the opposite. The less educated people who were hired to do the manual labor of setting up the stages, sound system and electronic components responded very well to touch. It worked especially well if the touch was accompanied with looking at the diagrams of how the room was to be arranged.

Two other ways that physical presence can influence another person's metabolism are the refinement techniques of 90° and Neutral.

Refinement: 90° and Neutral

1-27

What can a communicator do when she approaches a person and that individual suddenly holds his breath or begins to breathe higher than the communicator desires?

As soon as the person starts to breathe high, the communicator wants to stop and look at a third point (e.g., a paper). This is best done when the communicator is to the side of the person, but it is also okay to be at a 90° body angle.

The communicator wants to avoid being directly in front of the person. If the person is holding his breath, wait a moment. Whenever a person is holding his breath, the state is referred to as neutral (rather than *receptive* or *unreceptive*). There isn't enough oxygen to the brain for the person to think clearly—even the person doesn't yet know what his own response will be.[13] Once he starts to exhale, the communicator can approach, looking at the work in front of the person.

Pattern 8. Decontamination

1-28~32

We have all found ourselves in a situation where we have had to deliver unpleasant news. And we felt in a bind as if we had to choose between being nice and being honest. The Decontamination pattern gives us the specific behaviors that will let us be both nice and honest when delivering unpleasant news.

Decontamination is a process whereby two concepts are separated from each other by having each concept associated with a different location. This is especially helpful when the communicator wants to broach a difficult topic and still keep the other positive topics from being contaminated. How does decontamination work? It works through our systematic use of a curious and universal phenomenon: literally, locations have memories.

Location has memory

To verify for yourself that "location has memory," think of a time when you were somewhere in your home, say the living room, and you decided to get a glass of water from the kitchen. As you got up and were walking to the other room, an object—e.g., a misplaced key on an end table—distracted you. After picking the key up and reflecting back on how you might have inadvertently left the key there, you continue toward the kitchen but cannot remember why you were headed in that direction. As silly as it seems, by going back to the living room chair and sitting down (I hate to think that is where my brain is located), the memory of why you were headed toward the kitchen returns.

8

Decontamination is more than the use of multiple locations associated with different concepts. Actually the association is between any set of non-verbals and a concept or memory. The more the non-verbals associated with one concept or memory are different from the non-verbals associated with another concept or memory, the more the concepts and memories are distinguished from each other. Examples of non-verbals include:

- Location (for example: at home compared to at the office, indoors compared to outdoors, front of the room compared to back of the room)

- Voice (for example: approachable compared to credible, fast compared to slow, loud compared to soft)

- Posture (for example: leaning forward compared to leaning backward, standing compared to sitting, elbow on table compared to elbow not on table)

- Props (for example: glasses on compared to glasses off, folder open compared to folder closed, holding pen compared to not holding pen)

An example of non-verbals being associated with a concept or memory is when we are grocery shopping and unexpectedly bump into a colleague from work. We embarrassingly can't recall the colleague's name. This is because we are not surrounded by the non-verbals of work.

> *Non-verbals have memory.*

1-33

Refinement: Moving and Verbal Pretense

The transition from one location (associated with a concept or memory) to another location (associated with another concept or memory) involves several skills. Pattern 18 explains how to *connect* the locations associated with the different concepts and memories. Pattern 19 explains how to *separate* the locations associated with the different concepts and memories.

When moving from one location to a new location, the audience often needs a verbal pretense to explain why the communicator is walking to a different area; for example, the communicator could say something like, "Before we begin..." When the communicator is returning to an already established location, no verbal pretense is needed.

1-34

Refinement: Linking

Once two or more locations are established, they can either be linked together or collapsed into one another. Linking is accomplished when the locations are consistently referred to, both verbally and non-verbally, in a given sequence. This gives the listeners an impression of the concept associated with one location triggering/causing/affecting the concept associated with the other location.

When a teacher wants students to raise their hands, the teacher says, "Raise your hand if you know…" The instructor models by raising her hand. The pupils link the verbiage (i.e., "Raise your hand if you know…") with the non-verbal signal of the teacher's raised hand. By the time the teacher has said the verbal with the non-verbal modeling a few times, the linkage is so strong that the teacher can ask a question and just non-verbally model "raise your hand" and the students will raise their hands.

8

One of the best sources to understand associating non-verbals with a concept is to study an effective minister. Notice how she associate*s* herself with the Bible. Observe when the preacher looks at (visual), speaks to (auditory), and touches (kinesthetic) the Bible, thus linking the Bible to herself.

Refinement: Collapsing

1-35

Once two or more locations or sets of non-verbals have been established, the locations or sets of non-verbals can be collapsed. In the following example, the speaker joins two subgroups of people into one larger group. The members will then identify more with each other. When a group is cohesive, accelerated learning can occur.

> *The more people identify with one another the more their learning will be accelerated.*

An example of collapsing is when a speaker opens the seminar by asking, "Which of us are from out of town?"

The speaker raises her right hand as this question is asked. This hand then represents those participants who traveled. Then the speaker lowers the right hand a little and asks, "And which of us are local?" and raises her left hand. The speaker now has the two populations represented by her two raised hands. When the speaker says, "Let's welcome our out-of-town guests" and leads the applause by bringing her hands together, the two groups are symbolically collapsed into one unified group.

Refinement: Sorting to Increase Your Energy

One reason for Decontamination's popularity is that by decontaminating her world the communicator has a dramatic increase in energy.

The concept of decontaminating to increase the communicator's energy can take several forms, but all have the same underlying principle. That is, use non-verbals to separate troublesome items from other items.

One method of using non-verbals to separate items is "sorting" tasks. Think of a stack of papers that are reminders of "work to be done." If there is a particularly difficult task in the stack, the whole stack seems overwhelming. Remove the troublesome item from the stack and put it someplace else; wherever the troublesome item is placed, that location will be associated with "being difficult." By separating out the troublesome item, the original stack now seems "do-able." Using different locations increases our energy by containing the troublesome items in a location away from the rest of the items.

Eating and Sleeping

One of the most important areas to decontaminate is our home. This is because our home is where we recharge our batteries so we can return to work refreshed. We want to localize where we keep "professional-world" responsibilities.

There is a story of a French painter who used the back of his home as his studio. He wisely boarded up the passage between his living quarters and his studio. Every morning after breakfast he would leave his home through the front door, walk around the block, and enter his "back" door—the door to his studio.

Anyone who has ever worked on a master's degree can report how the dining room table becomes the reference library. The home is filled with the non-verbals of the final paper/project. The home has been contaminated.

The two places in the home that we want to keep as pleasant experiences are where we eat and sleep. It is important that those two areas not be contaminated with negative content. For many families the only consistent time that all members are present is when they are at the dining table; hence, often this is where the king and queen respond to requests from their royal subjects. With all the concerns over eating disorders, there is no need to associate food with less-than-pleasant content.

The second area to monitor so that we have greater energy is our nightstand. Only allow for comforting or pleasant/fantasy materials. For some of us this might be an inspirational book such as the Bible.

I can program my sleep to be more restful by having only enjoyable reading material on the nightstand. In my fantasy world I secretly own several professional sports teams and therefore have to read the sports section of the USA TODAY newspaper so that I am informed as I make my major decisions. Grappling with fantasy trades and coaching strategies creates a relaxing break from my day-to-day responsibilities.

Time-out

The major benefit of decontaminating is an increase in energy because certain activities are only done in certain locations. When a negative thing is done in one location and the person leaves that location, the negative association with that activity is left behind. The concept of "Time-out" fits such a description. If the parent consistently has the child stand in a given corner of a room when being told to reflect on his behavior, then that time-out spot is associated with management. When he leaves the corner, the management is over and the child has a fresh start.

Vignette: Mobile "Time Out"

One of the thrills of being a grandparent is to witness our offspring's rendition of how they think we raised them. As our daughter and son-in-law entered the front door for an afternoon and evening with us, I noticed what looked like a rolled up throw rug tucked under Mark's arm. My curiosity was interrupted with a joyous hug from my two and a half year old grandson. After-dinner activities included grandpa's back providing horse rides and grandma doing rounds of "tickle-monster." At some point little Calvin's energy was waning and he did a normal inappropriate behavior. Mark wisely unrolled the blue throw rug and put it in the corner. When Calvin was warned to change his behavior and when he didn't, he was given time-out on the rug. I sat there and marveled at their parenting skills. I reflected back on all the times I, as a parent, had visited family and friends and lost the routines that our kids were used to at home but didn't have available elsewhere. But here before my very eyes was the answer—a portable non-verbal—a throw rug.

Pattern 9. Frozen Hand Gesture

1-36~38 **9**

Patterns 9 through 12 address the arena of gesturing.

"What is the best starting point for learning non-verbal communication?" This is the most common question that ambitious people ask me. The answer is always the same...begin by increasing your ability to pause. The most common way to effectively pause is to do so with a Frozen Hand Gesture.

First a note on why the pause is the most essential aid to effective communication. Effective communication is interspersed with the pause. The pause is omnipresent. While the pause could be a part of every pattern, it is an especially integral part of the following Pentimento patterns:

• Transitions Between Points of Focus, Pattern 2.

• The transitions between the Credible and Approachable Voice Patterns, Pattern 4.

• The transition from the "ABOVE" to the "whisper," Pattern 6.

- The separation of two different sets of non-verbals (e.g., location) when doing a Decontamination, Pattern 8.

- Frozen Hand Gesture, Pattern 9.

- Gesturing: Assigning Attributes, Pattern 11.

- High Expectations, Pattern 13.

- Pause, Breathe and Join, Pattern 18.

- Break and Breathe, Pattern 19.

- The transitions between Voice Patterns and Breathing, Pattern 20.

- Pause and Look Intelligent, Pattern 21.

The pause is placed here because the Frozen Hand Gesture is the most common kinesthetic non-verbal which accompanies the pause. Using the Frozen Hand Gesture holds the listener's attention during the pause. Although the listener usually does not look at the communicator's frozen hand during the pause, the Frozen Hand Gesture still occupies the listener's attention. Mastering the Frozen Hand Gesture is the number one skill from which you can build your repertoire of competencies.

How is the Frozen Hand Gesture done? Like most elegant strategies, it is simple but not easy. As will be elaborated in Patterns 18, 19, and 21 effective oral communication is a combination of talking and pausing. To fully appreciate the impactfulness of the Frozen Hand Gesture you might want to jump ahead to those patterns now. The Frozen Hand Gesture is most often done during the pause. To use a Frozen Hand Gesture, you must first be gesturing while talking. Then every time you pause, simply freeze your hand gesture. Don't move your hand until the precise moment you resume talking.

Pattern 10. Gesturing: Four Quadrants

1-39

The Pentimento opened with Points of Focus—most people's favorite pattern. "Gesturing: Four Quadrants" is the kinesthetic equivalent of the visual Points of Focus.

So think about it. You have found profit in using two-point and three-point communication systematically. Why not add gesturing to your repertoire of two- and three-point communication?

Points of Focus and Decontamination introduced the concept of using locations systematically. This pattern expands the concept by identifying the locations the communicator can gesture toward. There are two ways of describing those areas. The first way is used more in a group setting, the second way is often used in a one-on-one setting. The difference between the two ways is how the fourth point is seen.

10

Gesturing in a Group Setting

In a group setting, there are four locations one can gesture toward. (The Points of Focus are in parenthesis.)

- Toward oneself (one-point)

- Toward the listener (two-point)

- Either side of the front of the room (three-point)

- Any reference to outside the room (four-point)

The following four scenes illustrate the four locations a speaker can gesture toward.

First Scene
I am so pleased

(one-point)

Second Scene
that you have traveled from far places to come here.

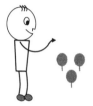

(two-point)

Third Scene
Our agenda has three major points.

(three-point)

Fourth Scene
Our revenue out there is down by 12%.

(four-point)

These intentional gestures can accompany the natural flow of speech as the speaker points to himself (one-point), gestures toward the audience (two-point), points to something close by, for instance a flipchart (three-point), or refers to something outside the room (four-point). The graphic below illustrates these four points.

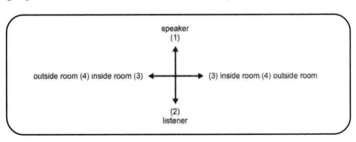

Gesturing in a One-On-One Setting

The second way of describing the four locations is:

- Toward oneself (one-point)

- Toward the listener (two-point)

- Toward a visual representation that is close to the speaker and listener (third-point)

- Toward the area that is farther from the speaker and listener (four-point)

The fourth point is any distance away from where the speaker and listener are. The fourth point could be outside the room (as described in the "Gesturing in a Group Setting") or it could be inside the room.

10

In the following aerial diagrams, two people (Person A and Person B) are having a debrief meeting. Person A has just finished a presentation. The two are seated at a table at the back of the room. The audience has left. Person A asked Person B to do an observation of three skills that Person A wanted to practice during the presentation. Person B is about to give Person A the feedback. Person B will be the speaker. Person B's observation notes are on the paper on the table.

The following four scenes illustrate the four locations a speaker can gesture toward.

Person B can gesture toward the following locations:

- toward herself (a one-point),

- toward Person A (a two-point),

- toward the paper (a three-point), or

- back toward the presentation location (a four-point)

First Scene
Thank you for asking me...

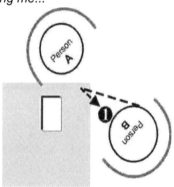

Second Scene
...to watch you during the presentation you just made.

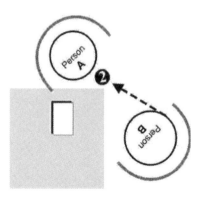

Third Scene
Here is the feedback on the three skills you wanted to practice.

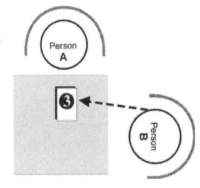

Fourth Scene
Remember when you were standing by the flipchart and Frank asked the question...

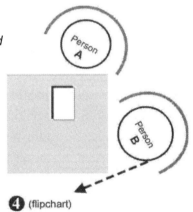

10

The graphic below summarizes gesturing in a one-on-one setting.

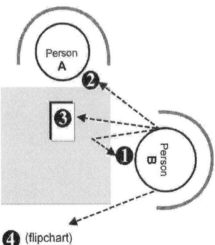

The benefit of using the four gesturing locations is detailed in Pattern 11.

Pattern 11. Gesturing: Assigning Attributes

1-40

Pattern 10 introduced us to gesturing in four locations. We are now ready to use the locations in a practical manner. Besides gesturing to hold the listener's attention, we can use gestures to assign attributes. The guidelines for assigning attributes—positive or negative—are the same when using Points of Focus. Attributes can be assigned (or said) by gesturing to oneself, toward the listener, toward content at a third point, or reference something farther away. It would be ideal to have the negative assigned outside the room (four-point), that would keep the environment inside the room positive. However, there are many times when it is necessary to have the negative inside the room. When this is the case, assign the negative to a third point (e.g., flipchart).

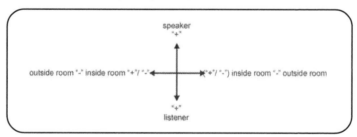

Assigning attributes is most easily done in stories and metaphors. For example if the following message were said,

> "Einstein was a genius. In his mental experiments he could think of phenomena which were com-

pletely inaccessible to the normal mortals out there,"

several attributes could be assigned. For example,

> "Einstein [*speaker points to herself*] was a genius
> [*points to listeners*]. In his mental experiments
> [*points to flip chart with the agenda*] he could think
> [*points to her head*] of phenomena which were com-
> pletely inaccessible to the normal mortals out there."
> [*looks and gestures outside the window*].

In these two sentences the speaker gets some of Einstein's
fame by pointing to herself when mentioning his name and
by pointing to her head when saying "think." The listeners
feel like geniuses and that the content they are going to cover
has the high level of Einstein's mental experiments. The
audience also feels they are different from the average humans (normal mortals) out there who cannot reach such intellectual heights. All this happens on a subconscious level
because on the conscious level the words occupy the listeners' attention.

11

Grocery Aisle of Life

To appreciate the importance of this and the previous pattern, think of your experiences in the grocery aisle of life.
As you shop you notice someone you know walking down
one of the aisles. If the person's back is to you, you have the
choice of deciding whether or not to visit with the person.
There are numerous reasons why one makes this decision.
For our purposes we will focus only on one reason—whether
the person is a positive or negative-oriented person. That
is, do we feel better or worse after an interaction with this
person?

When we ask them, "How have you been?" the other person often gestures toward us as we listen. They especially gesture toward us as they say the most important parts of the conversation. If the person is positive oriented, we leave the interaction in a more positive mood because they gesture toward us as they share all the wonderful things in their life. With more negatively-oriented people, we often depart with less energy because they pointed to us as they shared all their negative things in their life.

For example as we listen to a positive-oriented person we are the recipients of wonderful attributes. If the statements were, "The sunset was beautiful…" "He is getting better and better every day…" or "The speaker was really intelligent…" we walk away with the attributes of "beautiful," "better and better," and "intelligent."

Likewise, when we listen to a negative-oriented person, we are the recipients of negative attributes. For example, if the statements were: "The traffic was terrible…" "The computer broke…" "The dress was ruined…" unconsciously we are *assigned* the attributes of "terrible," "broke," and "ruined."

It makes sense why we enjoy bumping into positive-oriented friends—we leave those interactions with more energy.

Vignette: RIF

As Ifram Abdul opens the annual meeting of district managers he smiles and welcomes them to the conference. After mentioning the hours and agenda for the next two days, Ifram walks to the outside wall and holds a sheet of paper off to the

> side. While looking at the paper he says in a stac-
> cato voice, "At some point, we will address the
> need to reduce our work force by 10%." As the
> managers hold their breaths, Ifram freezes. As they
> finally breathe Ifram sets the paper on a stool and
> returns to the middle of the front of the room.
> With a relaxed gesture and in a calm and confi-
> dent voice Mr. Abdul states, "We will find ways
> to deal with [*he turns and gestures toward the
> stool and raises his voice*] THAT!"

In the vignette Ifram effectively separates the location of
the negative (at the stool) from the locations of the positive.

Opening Remarks

As speakers we have all found ourselves in front of a re-
sistant audience. At those times, we wish we could wave
a magic wand to get them into a different mental state—
like being "open," "curious," and "amazed." We have to
resist the temptation to shout, "Hey, come on! You need
to be *open* to these ideas, *curious* about how to implement them, and *amazed* at the benefits you will receive
from utilizing them."

If we did that, the participants would probably resist even
more. Making people conscious of how they feel emotionally sometimes exacerbates the situation. An alternative is to do our *Opening Remarks* by telling a story in
which the key words (*opened, curious, amazed*) are said
and as they are spoken, the speaker gestures toward the
listeners to convey unconsciously that these *attributes* are
being *assigned* to the audience.

For example, the speaker could open the program with,

> "Thank you for coming. Our topic is Customer Service.
>
> Before we begin it might be *curious* for you to know where this research comes from.
>
> When I first *opened* the investigation into the best model to improve our Customer Service, I was *amazed* to learn ..."

As each attribute is said the speaker gestures to assign the attribute. A description of the attribute being assigned is in brackets.

> "Thank you for coming [*hand gestures toward the audience; second point*]. Our topic is Customer Service [*gesturing to a flipchart; third point*].
>
> "Before we begin [*as the speaker walks off to the side = "Verbal Pretense"*] it might be *curious* [*gesturing toward the audience*] for you to know where this research [*gesturing back to the area where the greeting was done and where the presentation will be*] comes from.
>
> When I [*gesturing to the listeners to indicate that in this section of the story the word "I" is actually referring to the group*] first *opened* [*gesturing toward the audience*] the investigation into the best model to improve our Customer Service [*gesturing to the flipchart*], I was *amazed* [*gesturing to the group again*] to learn ..."

As a learner

Assigning Attributes

For the next two weeks, when you talk to others notice how you naturally gesture as you share the most important parts of your story. Then notice how often you mention positive attributes and how often you mention negative attributes. This will provide you with data on how others might see you as positive-oriented or negative-oriented.

During this same two-week period, when you are listening to others notice how they also naturally gesture when they share the most important parts of their story. Notice how often they mention positive or negative attributes. This will provide you with feedback on which people you enjoy being around.

Pattern 12. Gestures of Relationship

12

1-41

The relationship level of communication affords us the greatest flexibility. This pattern speaks to the non-verbals that foster this level of communication. When we gesture back and forth between ourselves and the listener, we silently indicate that a relationship is being fostered or that we already have a relationship and it is being called upon.

> ### Vignette: "...and Carl said..."
>
> I once was invited to address a group of humanists. Just before the presentation I was informed that an article had been circulated that attempted to put a negative slant on an organization (NLP) of which I was a member. I also knew that Carl

Rogers, who had personally trained me, was seen in a most favorable light by humanists.

During the opening I incorporated the following story. "…On one occasion a group of particularly bright people [*I swung my gesture throughout the audience to indicate that they were that "particularly bright people"*] had gathered to listen to Carl Rogers [*I turned sideways, pointed and looked at a spot to my immediate left*] talk. After a while a certain inquisitive person [*I pointed and looked at the most skeptical member of the front row*] asked Carl [*as this was said the gesture towards the skeptical person was moved to the Carl Rogers spot to my immediate left. As the gesture was moving towards the Carl spot, I turned and looked at that spot.*], 'What is the most important value that we need to take away from today?' [*After a pregnant pause I stepped into the spot and looked directly at the audience.*] And Carl said …"

Fisher and Ury in their seminal work, *Getting to Yes*, were among the first researchers to explain why the relationship level of communication provides the greatest options. When people are in a relationship, if they have a desire to preserve the relationship they are more likely to compromise on the issue level. Fisher and Ury delineated the three levels of communication as:

- The issues level
- The needs/motivation (behind the issue) level
- The relationship level

We want to operate on the relationship level of communication because of the additional options we get. One of the non-verbal ways to access the relationship level is to use gestures in a structured manner. This structured way of gesturing is called *Gestures of Relationships*. Once we have practiced the *Gestures of Relationship* there are three refinements that will add flexibility to our repertoire. The first refinement is written with a group in mind.

Refinement: Assuming Relationship

1-42

The communicator can shorten the time it takes to establish a relationship with a new audience by creating a location to represent a person that the group already associates with traits (e.g., "trust," "respect") they value. The communicator then steps into the location, assumes the phantom person's qualities and thus inherits a relationship with the listeners.

Vignette: Tom Clancy

Once on an Australian tour, I was slated to present to the faculty of the Australian equivalent of West Point and Annapolis. I was concerned that my lack of military background might put me at a disadvantage so in preparation I read *Patriot Games* in order to gather pertinent stories. As I presented, there were times when the audience's attentiveness would wane. At these times, I would walk over to the window and read relevant passages from Clancy's book. With the book directly between myself and the military brass present, I would open with, "Clancy [*I would touch my chest to indicate that I am Clancy*] says [*gesturing from my chest, briefly touching the book and finishing the gesture towards the audience*] to us. The following is a paraphrase of one of those passages: as I [*gesturing toward the audience*] lay in wait

12

> for the signal to advance, I reflected on how valuable it would have been had I [*again gesturing from the audience*] listened better to my instructors [*the gesture that had been extended towards the listener ends up returning to my chest*].

In essence, Michael Grinder might not have permission to directly tell them *to listen!* But Tom Clancy did. This example also illustrates Points of Focus, Decontamination, Assigning Attributes, Gestures of Relationship . Figuratively, from outside the room a phantom person of distinction—Tom Clancy—[*fourth point*] would look at the audience [*second-point*] and indicate that they needed to listen to the speaker [*one-point*]. By the third time that I walked over to the window, the professors sat up and eagerly awaited the next installment of their hero speaking directly to them. In time, I brought the book back to the center of the room. I became Clancy.

1-43

Refinement: Gestures of Reliance

The communicator can also create a desire within the listeners to get what is at the third point. By gesturing from the audience to the third point through herself, she nonverbally indicates that the she is avenue through which the group will obtain their "carrot."

As the next vignette illustrates, this concept of reliance on the communicator can work in both directions; the communicator can gesture from the third point through herself to the audience, thus non-verbally indicating that the third point is represented by her.

Vignette: TV Church

Preface: I am a great student of TV Church. As a culture the preachers have an excellent ability to pause with a Frozen Hand Gesture. So although the following example is from religion, it is not about religion; the reader is reminded that this work is a focus on the process level of communication. In no way do I mean to imply any opinion on the preachers' content. It is also important to state that what follows is an extrapolation of what the most skilled preachers frequently do.

The preacher extends his arms out toward his congregation and says, "We all want to get to heaven." As the word "heaven" is bellowed, the preacher moves his arms so that they point to the ceiling. By pointing up, he is shifting his arms from a second point of focus to a third point of focus. If, however, the preacher interjects a movement between the gesture toward the parishioners and the gesture toward the sky by having his arms touch his body as he looks down, he non-verbally indicates, "You get to heaven through me." This sequence of gestures—you...me...heaven—goes by quickly, but the message is unmistakable.

In a similar manner, the preacher could begin with his arms pointing to heaven while saying, "And the Lord said..." and then gesture toward the listeners as he says, "to us." The preacher is shifting from a third point of focus to a second point. If he gestures to himself in between the two focuses—God...me...you—he non-verbally conveys that he is the people's connection to the voice of God.

12

1-44

Refinement: Gestures of Onus

The third refinement is gestures that indicate whose responsibility/onus/burden it is to get to the third point. These gestures make it non-verbally clear who is responsible for getting results. There are three possibilities:

- Listener is responsible. Do this by gesturing toward the listener as the third point (task/result) is mentioned.

- Communicator is responsible. As communicator, gesture toward yourself as the third point is mentioned. (This is the same as the Gestures of Reliance concept; the communicator is the one who gets everybody to the desired goal.)

- Both listener(s) and communicator are responsible. Gesture back and forth between listener and communicator as third point is mentioned.

Vignette: Doctor, Patient and X-rays

As the doctor converses with the patient about the results of the examination, she empathetically explains that the patient has "x." The patient is shocked and momentarily stops breathing.

After the patient starts breathing again, the doctor wants to outline a plan of treatment in such a way that the patient is a full partner in his convalescence. What options does the doctor have to engage the patient in his recovery?

The doctor has three behavioral choices. (The following bullets correspond with the above three ways to indicate which party is responsible for results.)

- Patient is responsible. If the doctor does a Gesture of Relationship ending with the final thrust from the patient toward the patient's X-ray, the patient unconsciously feels emotionally abandoned. He has to fend for himself in his convalescence.

- Doctor is responsible. If the doctor ends the back-and-forth Gesture of Relationship by pointing to herself and she then transfers the gesture to the X-ray screen, the patient unconsciously feels he has a passive role in his recovery. What is conveyed is that the doctor is handling everything.

- Both are responsible. If the Gesture of Relationship finishes with the doctor's hand in the middle of the gesture loop before the hand extends to the X-ray, they both are joined in a plan of action. They will work together.

Pattern 13. High Expectations

1-45

13

Effective oral conversation includes both talking and pausing.[14] When someone is talking, the listener notices the communicator's culture; this includes the talking speed, volume, intonation and accent. In contrast, when a communicator pauses, the listener is impressed by the communicator's unspoken expectations. For example, something as simple as the position of the speaker's forearms can convey high expectations and belief in the listeners' self-reliance and potential to do well—or, it can convey the opposite. Unlike speech—which conveys information about a person's specific culture, the non-verbal behaviors during pauses in a conversation provide information that is cross-culturally true.[15]

My professional life encompasses both the corporate and educational worlds. I discovered how impactful a person's forearms are while I was coaching in schools. The classroom is a microcosm of what happens in the corporate world of communication. The difference is that teachers have more job security than most corporate managers. Job security plus the age difference between the teacher and her students results in the teacher operating with more autonomous power than do her corporate equivalents.

Because of how blatant education is about who is in charge, it is easier to observe the effect of a superior's influence on her subordinates. For example, when it comes to fostering autonomy and self-reliance in their subordinates, the people-in-charge may say all the right words. However, their non-verbal behaviors often send a different message, and those non-verbals speak volumes compared to the words spoken. What are the non-verbal behaviors that convey confidence and self-reliance in others?

While there are many non-verbals to watch for, what superiors do with their forearms and hands when they not gesturing is an easy way to assess superiors' level of confidence in their workers or their students. People who empower others to be autonomous and self reliant convey these high expectations by posturing their forearms in one of the three following positions:

1. Superiors keep their forearms waist-high in front of the body; wrists are at the same height as the elbows so that their forearms are parallel to the ground.

2. Or, superiors have both forearms at the side—hanging straight down.

3. Or, superiors have one forearm at their side and the other forearm at their waist, parallel to the ground.

All three convey the same message, "You (and we) are self-motivated and capable." When a communicator who has been silent decides to speak, the second and third positions allow the communicator to immediately gesture when speaking.

Vignette: Nat King Cole

One of my idols is Nat. His biography reveals what we all experience as we learn to be professional communicators. His musical career began as a pianist. One story goes that he was playing one night when the regular singer wasn't able to perform. An intoxicated patron demanded that the piano player sing—thus his serendipitous start. Old footage of his fame documents that at some point his popularity demanded that he stand and leave the ivory to someone else. He voiced how awkward he felt—he didn't know what to do with his hands. With practice he learned to keep one forearm at his side and the other forearm parallel to the ground, snapping his fingers in rhythm to the music. As he got to the peak points of the song, he intensified the climax of the music by gesturing with both hands.

13

From opera singers to actors in infomercials to effective ministers who don't use a pulpit—when not gesturing, all of them either hold their forearms parallel to the ground or have their forearms remain at their sides. Of course, they often do a combination of one forearm at the side and the other forearm parallel to the ground.[16]

One easy way of observing this phenomenon is to watch the newscasters. The anchors are seated at a counter with their wrists resting on the desk so their forearms are parallel to the ground.[17] As the station switches to an update from a reporter on the scene, watch how that person is holding her forearms. The clearest view of forearms being held in *high expectations* is provided when the weather person appears. She will be standing in front of a map with one hand at her side and the other hand holding an electronic pointer.

Object in Hand

A fascinating question arises. Can you "fake it 'til you get it?" In other words, if a communicator artificially does certain external behaviors (e.g., arms at side or waist-high and parallel to the ground) which are by-products of certain internal traits (e.g., high expectations), will this allow the communicator to eventually acquire the traits which will influence other people?"

YES!

How would someone who normally doesn't hold her forearms in the High Expectations posture learn to posture her forearms in the recommended way?

One way to learn how to hold your hands/forearms in the high expectations posture is to hold an object in your hand. Think of the last wedding you attended or look at some old wedding pictures. The bridesmaids hold flowers; hence, their forearms are parallel to the ground. When you compare the bridesmaids' posture with how the groom's party stands with their hands in the fig leaf posture, it is obvious who looks more intelligent and comfortable with themselves—the females.

As you practice holding an object, the object can be either held at your side or in the hand of the forearm parallel to the ground. If the object is held in the hand at your side, the object can be squeezed or twirled to release energy (e.g., anxiety). When holding the object in front, it is recommended that the object be held with the hand you gesture least with (i.e., for right handed people—the left hand). There are two reasons for this. First, as you gesture, your non-gesturing hand (e.g., left hand) is like home base and your gesturing hand has a harbor to come home to. Usually the gesturing hand (e.g., right hand) returns to the bottom of the (left) hand that stayed home. The second reason not to gesture with the hand holding the object is that it sometimes looks like the "pope with holy water blessing the crowd." The object is a symbol of the positional status of the communicator, so gesturing with an object conveys non-verbally, "I am in a higher position than you are."

We want to keep our forearms in the recommended position. It is helpful to know the five ways not to hold the forearms and what they convey. This knowledge allows us to vary our behavior when we are not getting the response we want.

13

Least Recommended Approachable Positions

Figleaf	**Pockets**	**Behind Back**

Least Recommended Credible Positions

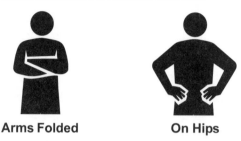

Arms Folded On Hips

Recommended Positions

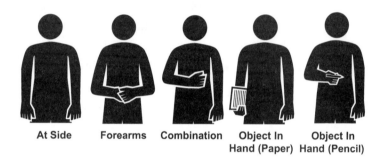

At Side   Forearms   Combination   Object In   Object In
Hand (Paper)   Hand (Pencil)

When subordinates see their superiors in a posture like any one of the first three pictures, the subordinates interpret the boss as communicating, "I hope you like me." The last two postures are interpreted by subordinates as, "You'd better fear me."

The picture of the person crossing her forearms across the chest is of special interest. Most books on non-verbal communication focus on others' non-verbals. This work prods us to focus on our own non-verbals. Other books teach the reader how to interpret others' intentions based on their non-verbals. The Pentimento encourages us to interpret our non-verbals by asking ourselves, "What meaning do others assign to *my* non-verbals?" We want to keep in mind what our intentions are when communicating as we simultaneously notice how others are responding.

In the picture of the person crossing her forearms across her chest, we see a posture that is often misinterpreted. She might be crossing her arms because she is cold yet her subordinates are likely to think she is operating from her position of authority.

Central to understanding Pentimento is the question, "Do we have to behave in a way that doesn't feel congruent? When do we get to be ourselves?" When things are going well we can be ourselves. When things are difficult Pentimento provides us with a proactive way of knowing how our non-verbals are likely to be interpreted. For those of us who are grappling with the question of our behaviors not seeming genuine and authentic, here are three reassuring comments:

- Sort out which situations are occasions where we are just self-expressing. In those situations we want to be associated and be very much ourselves.

- In other situations where it is important that our message be interpreted the way that we intend it to be interpreted, we want to be flexible in how we convey the message. If we realize that our non-verbals are likely to be misunderstood, Pentimento gives us choices to adjust our non-verbals so we can convey our intentions more accurately.

- The more we practice the various patterns, the more they become part of us; eventually, we will feel authentic and real in delivering them.

13

This pattern ends with a vignette that combines the skills of High Expectations and Frozen Hand Gesture.

Vignette: Fred

Fred was a most eager participant in a "presentation skills" seminar. Fred spoke with almost no gestures. At the same time he was convinced of the powerful effect of gestures and wanted to use gestures to emphasize the most important points of his delivery. He had two concerns. Both of them had to do with timing.

Fred spoke with his hands at his side. As Fred said an important point, he realized he wanted to punctuate the point with a gesture. The difficulty was, with his hands at his side, by the time his hand came up into a gesture position, his shorter, important points had already gone by. Fred solved this difficulty by holding his forearms parallel to the ground. With his hands at his waist, he could transition his hands into a gesture quickly.

Fred's second concern was learning how long to hold his hand in a Frozen Hand Gesture. The difficulty was that Fred would hold the gesture during the two or three seconds pause that followed his delivery of the most important point. Then he made his mistake: he would awkwardly drop the gesture at the end of the pause before he continued speaking. He knew that the dropping of the gesture was deleting the powerful effect he made just a second ago. He just didn't know the appropriate timing of when to stop the Frozen Hand Gesture and go back to his normal style of presenting without gesturing. He wanted to find a way of making the transition back to his forearms being at the parallel High Expectations position.

Through trial and error he discovered that he could hold his gesture during the pause following the important information until he started to speak about less important content. Then while speaking about the less important content he would retract his gesture, repositioning his hands at his waist. He was back in the High Expectations position ready to gesture when he came to his next important point.

Pattern 14. Kinesthetic Equivalents of Credibility and Approachability

1-46

Pattern 4 dealt with voice patterns. We know the concepts of credibility and approachability are important because of the high number of people who object to the connotation of these words. This is especially true for females. My six biological sisters have versed me well in the social inequality shown by the business world when it comes to promotions and in how, as the demarcation between genders has blurred, sometimes the male is still given preferential treatment. As previously mentioned, for example, the male (statistically associated with the credible end of the continuum) who exhibits approachable behaviors is often seen as a *sensitive, new age guy.* In essence, his gender appeal actually increases. A female (statistically placed at the approachable terminal) who exhibits credible behaviors is labeled with less than respectful terminology.

14

Pattern 4 established the importance of the concepts of credible and approachable voice patterns. What are the kinesthetic equivalents?

Credibility	Approachability
stillness	movement
weight on both feet	weight more on one foot
toes pointed ahead	fashion posture
hands on hips or forearms crossed	fig leaf, in pockets, or hands behind back
gestures with palms down	gestures with palms up
gestures go from the speaker toward the listeners; fingers flat	gestures come from the listeners to the speaker; fingers curled

TV

Traditionally, being feminine has been equated with being nice. A smile from a woman was expected but considered even more meaningful from a man because it was unexpected. It is more than just interesting to note that newscasters are making a dent in our stereotypes of genders. The major cities and networks have female anchors whose femininity is beyond question. This allows them to break bad news with a credible voice pattern and to do so without a smile. Using Marshall McLuhan's (*The Medium is the Message*) ideas, TV is a visual vehicle and the female reporter's femininity is secured by looks.

Proof of the need for the female to appear feminine is the role that most females have on the morning radio stations. The partnership of two people as DJs statistically reveals the male is the lead and the female has a lesser role; this often includes laughing at his jokes. One might postulate that since the medium of radio isn't visual, the listeners cannot see the woman's femininity, so she is relegated to a more traditional role. And although TV is allowing females to simultaneously be competent (somewhat of a synonym for credible) and feminine, the breakup of old stereotypes is still not seen as enough.

As a learner

Gender Correlations

Credibility and approachability are conveyed by many physical traits. Part of the reason females are associated with approachability is that they have greater joint flexibility than males. Try the following experiments:

1. Ask a room full of people to put their hands on their hips. Statistically, the men tend to have their wrists straight and the women have their wrists bent.

2. Ask a room full of people to hold their forearms parallel to the ground with one hand resting in the other hand at the waistline. Women tend to bend their wrists more than men. This information about kinesthetic equivalents of credibility and approachability allows the communicator to know how to mechanically increase or decrease others' perception of his or her level of credibility/approachability. For example, if others are seeing the communicator as more credible than the communicator intends, then the communicator can appear more approachable by bending wrists or joints in general (fingers, elbows, knees). If oth-

14

ers are seeing the communicator as more approachable than the communicator intends then the communicator can straighten the wrists and joints in general.

3. Ask a group of men and women to stand. Have the participants freeze and notice how their neighbors have the body weight distributed on their legs. Have the participants take two steps and stop. Again notice how the weight is distributed. Statistically, females tend to stand with their weight on one leg more than the other. Males have their weight more evenly distributed. Women don't have their weight evenly distributed and this unevenness, that people associate with women, makes them seem approachable.

For anatomical reasons males are correlated with being more credible and females are associated with being more approachable.

female with straight head and even weight distribution = credible

male with head tilt and uneven weight distribution = approachable

Chapter Four

Breathing Patterns B

Overview

Non-verbal communication is categorized by Visual, Auditory, Kinesthetic and Breathing patterns. The breathing patterns are the most sophisticated of the non-verbal communication categories. They warrant our patience as we learn them. There are five breathing patterns:

- Pattern 15, BLIP (Breathing Level Indicates Permission)—explains the highest level of our professional development—permission. (See page 4 for more details.) And what is amazing about the BLIP pattern is that it is cross-culturally accurate.

- Pattern 16, Indicators of Breathing—provides us with an objective method for observing our permission level and determining if another person's receptivity to us is high (the person's breathing is abdominal) or low (the person's breathing is shallow).

- Pattern 17, Influencing Another's Breathing—summarizes the most sophisticated of all the Pentimento Patterns. You are encouraged to attend a training where the techniques are demonstrated and you can receive guided practice.

———

To be respectful of gender equality and yet provide the reader with a fluid reading style, in this section the communicator is referred to by male pronouns and other people are referred to by female pronouns.

- Pattern 18, Pause, Breathe and Join—clarifies how to deliver information without overloading our recipients. This pattern points out how listeners have a fixed amount of separate bits of information that they can incorporate. However, Pause, Breathe and Join teaches us how to connect those bits so that more bits can be learned. This pattern facilitates accelerated learning.

- Pattern 19, Break and Breathe—offers the valuable technique of how to deliver volatile information. Break and Breathe and Pattern 8, Decontamination (See page 76 for more details) are our number one and number two patterns for containing and managing stress.

Pattern 15. BLIP (Breathing Level Indicates Permission)

1-47~48

Because breathing is always present, it is hard to detect. As Margaret Mead[18] said, "If a fish was an anthropologist, the last thing it would discover is water."

When a person steps out of his culture he often can see his own "water" better. The following passage by Stretton Smith[19] illustrates the difference between the WASP and the Hawaiian cultures' breathing patterns during prayer. The WASP missionaries needed to step out of their "water" in order to understand why the Hawaiians were not attracted to Christianity. Hawaiians were not attracted because the Christians didn't breathe abdominally deep when praying.

Perhaps you've visited (Hawaii) on vacation or lived there yourself and you already know that all

Caucasians are called *haoles*. Literally, *haole* applies to anyone who is not a native-born, pure Hawaiian. But its common usage refers to Caucasians. I was fascinated when I learned the derivation of the word, for it's not an altogether complimentary term... So, here's the story. Though some Hawaiians claim it's a myth, it nevertheless illustrates a very important point: the Hawaiian people were a praying people ... long before... Christianity. (They) would sit outside of their temple for a long period of time–in prayer–before ever going inside the temple. Then the worshipers would go inside, go up to the altar area, and once again pray for a long time–in order *to breathe life* into the prayer.

Can you feel the process of breathing life into a prayer? The phrase *the Spirit of God* can be translated as *the Breath of God.* You breathe in the spirit of God, which is why the Hawaiians felt it necessary to breathe life into their prayers. When the Hawaiians would observe the missionaries in prayers, however, they would see the Christians enter into their church, sit down, rapidly utter a few sentences, hastily say, "Amen," and then get up and leave. It appeared to Hawaiians that the Christians completed their prayers far too quickly. The Christians were called *haoles* because the word means *without breath*. Haoles were those who failed to breathe life into their prayers. By Hawaiian standards, their prayers lacked the Spirit of God.

15

The Hawaiians are aware of breathing. Whether or not a culture is aware of breathing, breathing is the invisible and yet omnipresent non-verbal element of communication. To enhance our intuitive understanding of why we are consciously or unconsciously attentive to breathing, we turn to medical research.

Studies show the correlation between breathing and the release of chemicals in the body. When we breathe shallow/high in the chest (as we do when we raise our voices), we release chemicals of "fight or flight." Hearing the raised voice also causes the listener to release chemicals of fight or flight.

Sometimes we must say something loudly, but if we follow the loud statement with a deep abdominal breath, we produce chemicals of calmness.[20] During our pause to take the deep breath, the listeners will take their cues from us and also breathe more deeply. When we find ourselves having breathed shallow/high, we can breathe even more deeply if we move our bodies as we take the deep breath.

Least Recommended:
Shallow Breathing

Recommended:
Deep Breathing

BLIP is the single most sophisticated Pentimento Pattern to observe because it is the only cross-culturally accurate indicator of the communicator's permission level with another person or group. When a person trusts a communicator, she will breathe abdominally/low. If a slight distrust arises, this will show up as a change of breathing.

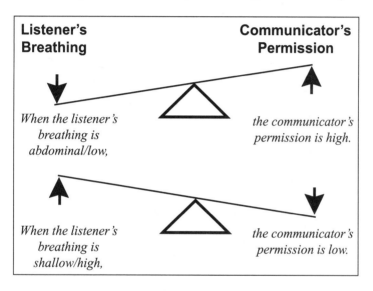

People who track aircraft with technical equipment watch the blips on screens. So while *BLIP* is an acronym, the term also suggests why the general population is so unaware of how to read the level of a person's receptivity. According to Diane Ackerman, the average breathing cycle is five seconds—two seconds to inhale and three seconds to exhale.[21] Shifts in breathing happen so quickly that the shift is like a quick, short blip. As daunting as the task is to increase one's ability to detect changes in breathing, it is also inspiring to realize that it is possible to see the things others miss. As Thomas Sowell says, "It takes considerable knowledge just to realize the extent of your own ignorance."[22]

15

I use electronic equipment to increase an observer's ability to notice breathing. In our "Perception Training" programs, we play at fast forward video footage of people talking. At such speed, the intervals between the inhalation and exhalation are shortened. This condensing allows the viewer to see the expansion and contraction of people's chests. Electronic viewing of communication reveals the breathing patterns of people. (See www. michaelgrinder.com for information on our training programs.)

As a learner

Inhale/Exhale Experiment One

To demonstrate the effect inhaling and exhaling has on a person's body, ask someone to join you for this activity. Respectfully explain the following procedure to the person. Ask the person to show you a tender spot on her back, usually between the shoulder blade and spine. Place your thumb gently on the tender spot. As the person inhales, increase the pressure on the spot; as the person exhales continue to touch the spot but return to the gentle level of contact. As the person inhales for a second time, increase the pressure on the spot. And during the exhale, return to gentle pressure. Memorize how that spot felt as you increased pressure during the two consecutive inhales.

Then change the sequence to compare how the chemicals are released during the inhalation and exhalation phases of the breathing cycle. This time, increase pressure on the spot during two consecutive exhales. That is to say, as the person exhales, increase the pressure and as the person inhales continue to touch but return to the gentle level of pressure. Repeat the process during the next breathing cycle. That is, as the person exhales, increase the pressure and as the person inhales continue to touch but return to the gentle level of pressure.

Switch roles and have the other person duplicate the exercise. Then discuss how the muscle feels during the exhalation compared to the inhalation. Is it more rigid or more supple during the exhalation?

If this exercise is done well, both persons will notice similar results. Dialogue to find out if both the sender and the receiver experienced the same increased physical ease during the exhalation as compared to the inhalation.

As a learner

Inhale/Exhale Experiment Two

To further increase your understanding of the chemical effects of inhalation vs. exhalation, do the following three stretching activities while in a sitting position.

- Hold your breath and slowly turn your head as far as you can to one side. Notice the farthest peripheral object that you can see. Return to looking straight ahead.

- This time, slowly turn your head to the same side while inhaling. Again, notice the farthest peripheral object that you can see.

- This time, slowly turn your head to the same side while exhaling. Notice the farthest peripheral object that you can see. Return to looking straight ahead.

15

Which phase of the breathing cycle allowed you to turn the farthest? Now repeat the same activity to the other side to see if the results are similar.

A question immediately arises: "Is the physical receptivity experienced in these activities indicative of mental receptivity also?" We are doing these breathing experiments to discover that our exhalation allows greater physical flexibility than our inhalation. Experiment Three will show that what occurs physically during the inhalation also occurs mentally. That is, the fight-or-flight chemicals that are released during the inhalation affect our hearing. We hear better during our exhalation.

 As a learner

Inhale/Exhale Experiment Three

Ask someone to join you for the following activity. Pretend you are showing her some new information on a piece of paper (third-point communication). When you have talked for three seconds, have the person suddenly sit straight up and hold her breath. When she holds her breath, it is a clear indication that she is breathing shallow/high. You will continue to talk as if you didn't notice that she shifted to shallow/ high breathing. Stop after 30 seconds. Switch roles and repeat the activity. Debrief by asking a question, "When you were holding your breath, how did that affect your ability to fully hear what was being said?"

When the listener begins to breathe high/shallow—or even more significantly, begins to hold her breath— we are wise to immediately stop talking. Why? For two reasons: 1) we have lost permission/receptivity and 2) even if the listener is trying to be receptive to us, she can't follow what is being said. Continuing to talk when the listener is not breathing well is ineffective and can often make things worse.

As a learner

Inhale/Exhale Experiment Four

So far we have experimented with the shallow/high breathing of the listener. This experiment focuses on how the communicator's response to the listener's shallow/high breathing can make the situation even worse.

This time, as you are talking, about three seconds into the activity, have the other person suddenly sit up straight holding her breath. Immediately switch from your three-point posture around to a two-point face-to-face and frantically say, "Are you OK?" Switch roles and repeat the activity.

Most people report that the quick appearance of the speaker's face (two-point communication) in front of the listener results in the latter gasping for more air… the shallow/high breathing only increases.

15

What is the recommended way of responding when a listener's breathing suddenly changes? When communicating in a three-point conversation, if the other person breathes shallow/high, stop talking. Remain still and silent as you continue to look at the third point, or, alternatively, shift your gaze to a fourth point. (Pattern 21 will teach us how to look intelligent during this pause.)

The Role of Exercise

Our lifelong goal is to breathe deep especially in pressure situations. Staying in oxygen shape is essential. Medical research shows that eating and sleeping properly will maintain our energy level. Exercise is the only proven way to increase our energy level; however, we are all susceptible to the syndrome of, "When my week gets busy, the first thing I drop is fitness." My dad always said, "It isn't the work that will kill you, it's the stress." Exercise is one of the best antidotes to stress because exercise allows us to breathe when under pressure.

Much of my last two decades have been spent living out of a suitcase. Frequently, I arrive at my destination after midnight. While my emotional self longs to sleep, my brain reminds me that I will be more successful the next day if I exercise for 20 minutes (often as simple as running in place in front of the TV). Intellectually, I know I want to provide others the highest form of service I can, and in order to do so I behaviorally need to release the chemicals that I get from exercising. I can almost hear the voice of my dad saying, "Twenty minutes of exercise is worth more than forty minutes of sleep."

Sometimes I have to set out my workout clothes before I leave for work in order to encourage myself to exercise when I finish my day. In addition to exercise the following are ways to practice breathing low and abdominal:

- Sing. Make a habit of singing when driving. Listening to music is worthwhile for many reasons, but to practice deep breathing don't just listen. SING! Of course, playing a wind instrument accomplishes the same thing.

- Laugh. (If interested, look at Norman Cousins' book on healing via laughing.)[23]

- Yawn. If you really want to take in oxygen do a *double yawn*: do a yawn and when the yawn is completed, continue to hold your jaw wide open. Then do an artificial second yawn by inhaling several gasps of air.

- Meditate, pray, do yoga or Tai Chi.

Our brain separates us from the rest of the primates. While the brain weighs only three to four pounds, it consumes from 25 to 37% of all oxygen inhaled. When we breathe high or shallow, the organs that rely most on oxygen, mainly the brain, are most affected. By practicing breathing low and deep via the above activities, we condition our bodies to better convert oxygen from our respiratory system into our circulatory system; we deliver more oxygen to our brain.

A communicator can have all the appropriate outcomes and be versed in many techniques, but if the communicator isn't breathing well enough such skills are for naught. And, of course, by breathing low and deep the communicator influences others to breathe low and deep also.

15

Behavioral Ethics

I was raised in a wonderfully religious household, spending the first two years of college in a seminary. Ethics is part of my fiber.

After college, I was professionally influence by the humanistic likes of Carl Rogers, Syd Simon, Harvey Jackins, Victor Frankl and the California culture of personal growth. I was part of "chicken soup" before it left the can and became a book.[24] My goal was to unconditionally accept someone—I could love the person into becoming all that she could be. I operated from the ethical consideration of intentionality. When interactions with others didn't go well, my first reaction was to go inside myself and ask, "What were my intentions? Did I have the other person's interest in mind?" If needed, my adjustments were intrapersonal. That is, I altered my attitudes, beliefs and perceptions.

While not replacing an ethics based on intentionality, I would like to add an ethics based on external behaviors. This work proposes an additional standard of ethics, one based on external behaviors. When a communicator interacts with a person, the person might breathe high or shallow. The more serious the situation, the more breathing is affected. If the communicator could have fulfilled his responsibility with the person breathing lower and deeper then the communicator wasn't as ethical as the communicator could have been.

The following is an example of behavioral ethics. A dentist is filling a patient's tooth while the patient is reclined in the chair. If the dentist mentions to the patient that she could use a cosmetic crown on a different tooth and she breathes shallow/high, the dentist isn't behaving as ethically as he could be. By contrast if, when he is finished with the treatment, she is in the upright position, the dentist comes around to the front of her and talks about the possibility of a cosmetic crown, she will statistically breathe deeper/lower. The reason for the variation in breathing is when the patient is in the prone position she expected service, not advice, information, or persuasion. The dentist contaminated his relationship with the patient by mixing up the location for treatment with the location for decision-making. (See Pattern 8.)

Pattern 16. Indicators of Breathing

Most doors operate on hinges. There is a hinge on the door and a hinge on the door frame. The pin that holds everything together is called a linchpin. Pattern 15 is the macro linchpin of permission; it explains *why* we want to be attentive to breathing. *BLIP* introduced us to the cross-cultural insight that people's breathing level indicates our level of permission with them. Pattern 16 provides us with the micro tools that show us how to observe the breathing of others.

There are four variables of the breathing cycle:
  The depth of the breathing cycle:
      1. shallow/high
      2. abdominal/low
  The phase of the breathing cycle:
      3. inhaling
      4. exhaling

The variables are closely related. Pattern 15 taught us that high/shallow breathing releases chemicals of fight or flight and abdominal/low breathing releases chemicals of calmness. Patterns 16 adds that every inhalation also releases chemicals of fight or flight and every exhalation releases chemical of calmness. The highest release of fight-or-flight chemicals is during the inhalation of shallow/high breathing; conversely, the greatest activation of calm chemicals is during exhalation of deep breathing. This is why during childbirth the expectant mother is trained to emphasize the exhalation. It is also understandable why Olympic weight lifters artificially increase their strength by sucking in gasps of air (inhaling) just before lifting the weights.

16

For a number of reasons, it is not practical to look directly at someone's chest to observe that person's breathing pattern. But we can figure out how the person is breathing by being attentive to the by-products of that person's breathing.

1-49

What are the indicators or byproducts of shallow/high and abdominal/low breathing?

When person is	Indicators of Shallow/High Breathing	Indicators of Abdominal/Low Breathing
moving	jerky	fluid
talking	"Uh!"	fluidity of finding words
reposing	stiff	still

1-50

What are the most obvious indicators of inhaling and exhaling?

Person's	When Inhaling	When Exhaling
head	moves back	moves forward
shoulders	move up and back	move down and cave
clothes	smoothed out	wrinkled

Some people find it helpful to do the following refinements:

• Our eyes see movement better when we are not looking right at the moving object. Look at the person's face and peripherally notice how the person's head, shoulders and clothes indicate that person's inhalation and exhalation.

- Look at a person's profile. On the far wall find a spot just in front of the person's face. Focusing on that spot, notice how the person's head moves. As the person exhales her head moves forward covering the spot on the wall. Likewise, when she inhales, her head moves back, revealing the spot.

- When a person talks, the person is exhaling. This fact allows us to get in sync with breathing even when communicating over the phone. As you are listening to someone who is upset, move your head forward when she is talking. Move your head back when she is not talking/pausing. Simply put, your head is in rhythm with her breathing. You have successfully *paced* her breathing. The next pattern explains how to use this information.

As a learner

Breathing and Peripheral Sight

Peripherally seeing another person's breathing is one of the most sophisticated skills of the Pentimento Patterns. Pattern 3 introduced the concept of Peripheral Sight. To practice peripherally seeing and to test the concept of seeing movement peripherally, do the following. Find a partner and arrange the two chairs so that your partner is looking straight ahead and you are sitting at a 90° angle looking directly at your partner. (Suggestion: ask your partner to close her eyes.) Looking directly at your partner's chest, notice the changes during inhale and exhale cycles. Actually see the chest cavity expand and contract. Gradually just look at your

16

partner's face and peripherally continue to notice the by-products mentioned in the previous chart (movement of head and shoulders, wrinkling of clothing).

Howard Gardner's seminal work on *Multiple Intelligences* offers a concept that sheds light on any discussion about observation. Gardner talks about *intrapersonal intelligence* and *interpersonal intelligence*. The first is how well one is in touch with one's inner self. This is one of the primary goals of personal growth work—to increase one's awareness of his own intuition. People who are right brained have and value this ability; such people are often described as being highly associated. Gary Larson, the creator of *The Far Side*, when asked where he gets his ideas, answers, "I don't know, but they better keep coming because I have deadlines."[25] The second intelligence, Gardner's *interpersonal intelligence*, is a focus outside oneself, to notice others. This external focus is frequently referred to as being dissociated. It is a state of non-possessive observation.

I strongly recommend that the practice of the two intelligences, interpersonal and intrapersonal, not be undertaken at the same time. To *see* (interpersonal) and then *feel* (intrapersonal) about what I just saw is the most dangerous of all observations—if for no other reason than while one is inside himself there are tremendous changes occurring outside that he is unable to observe; he is missing chunks of reality. Save the luxury of hallucinating what it means for those times when you are not in reality—like when doing daily exercises.

The purpose of observation is to accurately interpret what we see. In the case of breathing, it is the four variables of breathing: high and low breathing; inhalation and exhalation. In our Perception Training Program, we say, "If you can see half of what you are looking at, you are good. If you know which half to look at, you are a genius."

> *If you can see half of what you are looking at, you are good.*
> *If you know which half to look at, you are a genius.*

Pattern 17. Influencing Another's Breathing

1-51~53

Pattern 15 convinced us of the need to be attentive to breathing in order to gauge how receptive the other person is at any moment in time. Pattern 16 explored how to observe a person's breathing and told us what to watch for. Pattern 17 delves into how to use the observation. If the person is breathing well, then there is no need to influence the person's breathing. However, if the person is breathing too shallow/high then we want to influence the person to receive more oxygen because when we and the other person have enough oxygen to the brain, the interaction will be both more enjoyable and productive. This is true whether it is a social chit-chat or a heavy negotiation.

17

The Pentimento is a behavioral model rather than a psychological model. The difference between the models surfaces when observing someone who is not breathing abdominally deep. The psychological model would have us ask, "Why is the person not breathing deeply?" The psychological model is more sophisticated and complex than the behavioral model. I ask the psychological question of "why" when I have more time to reflect on what happened. Often this is after the interaction.

While interacting, I ask the behavioral question, "How can I influence this person to breathe deeper?" The behavioral model provides me with my immediate goal. When interacting, the behavioral model keeps me more present.

We can influence a person to breathe abdominal/low by employing the simple method, the sophisticated method, or a combination of the two.

Simple Method

1-54

The easiest way to influence another's breathing is to let our voice get slower and softer as we speak. The movie *Deep Impact* illustrates this simple method; in fact, movies are a great source for studying non-verbal communication. The following vignette is similar to the anecdote supplied in Pattern 5 ABOVE (Pause) Whisper—*Good Will Hunting*.

Vignette: Deep Impact (a movie)

An international group of astronauts are on a mission to plant explosives on a gigantic asteroid that is rapidly approaching Earth. They have to finish their work during the night because when the sun rises there will be a huge increase in the surface temperature, threatening their safety. Robert Duval is in command. As the sun starts to come over the horizon, he has to make life and death decisions. As the astronauts precariously return to the ship amid exploding volcanoes, one member of the crew is hurled into outer space. One of the returning astronauts, a Russian, confronts

Duval, yelling that the member who was left outside must be rescued. While the commander
emotionally aches for the lost companion, he also
knows that such an attempt would jeopardize the
entire crew. Robert calmly repeats, "Sit down, we
will be all right." Because Duval keeps his voice
slow and soft the Russian's metabolism finally
slows down. As oxygen returns to everyone's
brains, the tragic death is reluctantly accepted.

Sophisticated Methods

1-55

Auditory Method

As the other person inhales, be silent. Talk only as she
exhales. This technique is the auditory method of influencing another person's breathing.

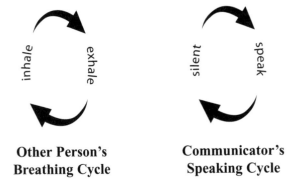

**Other Person's
Breathing Cycle**

**Communicator's
Speaking Cycle**

To do the sophisticated method of influencing another's
breathing (speaking only during the other person's exhalation), the communicator wants to:

17

• Speak only during the other person's exhale. As
the other person's head is moving forward, gradually talk even more softly and more slowly. This
is a combination of the simple and sophisticated
methods of influencing another's breathing.

- As the person exhales, move your head slightly forward toward the person. As the person inhales, move your head back. By having your head in sync with the other person's breathing your timing of speaking during the other person's exhale will be more exact. You may want to practice doing this "in-sync" movement in silence. When you have mastered moving your head in sync with the other person's breathing, then train yourself in the sophisticated auditory method. That is, you talk as you move your head forward (which is during the person's exhalation) and you are silent when moving your head backward (which is during the person's inhalation).

- Be silent when the other person's head is moving up and back.

- Stay away from questions.

- Stay away from sentences with action.

So far, the presented method for influencing a person's breathing has been to use our voices in a simple or sophisticated manner, or better yet, a combination of both. In addition to using this auditory method, we can also use visual and kinesthetic methods to influence a person's breathing.

1-56~58

Refinement: Visual Method

In the auditory method, we influence another's breathing with our words. In the visual method, we influence breathing by moving our body in sync with the other person's breathing cycle. Initially, we will combine the auditory and visual methods. Then we will practice using the visual method in silence (see p. 136, "When Listening").

As a learner

Review the Auditory Method

Sit so the listener can't see you but you can see the listener's breathing. As introduced on p. 131, talk as the person exhales. Remember to move your head slightly toward the person during her exhale. Move your head back as the person inhales. Keep your head in sync with the other person's breathing.

As a learner

Combine the Auditory and Visual Methods

Now sit so you and the listener can see each other. Do the sophisticated auditory method (talking only during the person's exhale) and the visual method (moving your head toward the person as the person exhales and moving your head back as the person inhales.)

Debrief: You have done the sophisticated auditory method twice. Once without the listener seeing you and once with the listener seeing you. The question is, "Did the listener's ability to see you move forward and backward (i.e., visual method) add to the effectiveness of the auditory method?"

Responding to Rapid Breathing

The extreme end of shallow breathing is rapid breathing. If the other person is breathing very rapidly (e.g., hyper), often you, as the communicator, cannot talk and breathe in sync with the listener because you will lose your own oxygen. The number of words you can say during her rapid exhalation is very few, so using the auditory method of

17

talking slow and low during her exhalation isn't practical. This is when you need to add the visual and/or kinesthetic methods. (See pages 132 and 138.)

To understand the effect of rapid breathing, compare rapid breathing to deep breathing and average breathing. A deep breathing pattern (see the left side of the following graphic) is comprised of three stages: inhale, exhale and pause. During the inhalation, chemicals of "fight or flight" are released. During both the exhalation and pause stages, chemicals of calmness are released. Think of a baby sleeping. You see the movement of the inhalation and the exhalation and then there is no movement. The "no movement" is the pause. Simply put, a breathing cycle has an inhalation, exhalation and a pause. During both the exhalation and the pause, chemicals of calmness are released. During an average breathing cycle (see the right side of the graphic), the pause disappears, which means that the fight-or-flight chemicals released are at least equal to, if not greater than, the calmness chemicals released. As previously mentioned, Diane Ackerman says that the average breathing cycle is five seconds—three seconds of inhalation and two seconds of exhalation.[26]

Books on meditation[27] recommend that you do four counts (i.e. seconds) for your inhalation and eight counts of exhalation.

During a rapid breathing pattern the person emphasizes the inhalation more than the exhalation. This results in the person releasing more chemicals of "fight or flight" than chemicals of calmness.

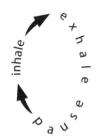

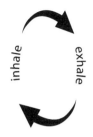

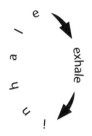

Deep/Abdominal Breathing Cycle	**Average Breathing Cycle**	**Rapid Breathing Cycle**
Releases More Calmness Chemicals	Releases Almost Equal Chemicals	Releases More Fight-or-Flight Chemicals

As a learner

Responding to Rapid Breathing

Sit so you and your partner can see each other. When initially learning this skill have your partner breathe a little more rapidly than normal. Eventually have your partner breathe very rapidly.

Because your partner is breathing rapidly you will talk continuously, breathing only once for the other person's two to four breathing cycles. By using the visual method of moving your head in sync with her breathing, your movement is affecting your voice and her breathing. Remember to have your voice be a pinch faster and louder when your head is fully back (i.e., when you first start to speak). As your head moves forward, your voice slows down and becomes softer. In other words, as she begins her exhalation she hears your "a-pinch-faster-and-louder" voice, then as she continues to exhale, your voice slows down and becomes softer.

17

You are talking continuously throughout her first, second and perhaps third breathing cycles. You have taken your cues from the other person. You have been in sync with the other person. Your head movement and voice have *paced* her breathing. During either her third or fourth inhalation, you will also inhale.

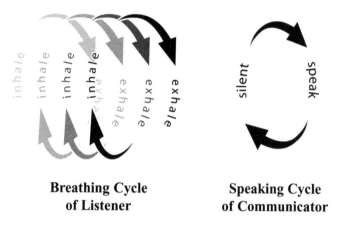

**Breathing Cycle
of Listener**

**Speaking Cycle
of Communicator**

You are now ready to *lead*. You want the other person to take their cues from you. You want them to be in sync with you. This time, when she stops her exhalation, you continue a pinch longer to move your head forward with your voice being slow and low. This influences her to hesitate longer before she begins her inhalation. You have influenced the other person to elongate her exhalation thus releasing more chemicals of calmness.

When Listening

The visual pace-lead is done when both parties can see each other. In the above example you were the speaker. Can the visual pace-lead method be used when you are the listener? Yes. It is helpful to realize that when someone is speaking they are exhaling. When someone pauses in her speaking, the person is most likely inhaling.

For instance, if someone is yelling at you, you could look at the yeller (two-point) when she starts to speak (exhale). As the yeller continues speaking during the same breath, you lower your head to a one-point. This simple action of moving from eye contact to looking down on every exhalation helps a yeller calm down and breathe better.

If this pacing doesn't shift her, then change to leading. That is, intentionally change your pattern. The possibilities are endless:

- Don't look up. Continue to look down.
- Abruptly shift your body.
- Do an "ABOVE, (Pause) Whisper."

17

If the person is yelling about something you did or failed to do, your permission is low and most likely the technique of pacing-leading won't work.[28]

Over the Phone

When listening over the phone to someone who is upset, she can't see your visual method of pace-lead. However, you still want to pace/move your head while listening. Move your head forward when she talks (exhales) and move your head back when she is silent (most likely inhaling).

This movement allows you to memorize the cadence of the person's breathing pattern. Then when it is your turn to speak you will speak with the same movement that you have memorized. You speak as your head comes forward and pause when your head moves back. Now you are ready to lead. Each time you speak with your head moving forward wait a pinch longer (i.e., continue to speak) before you pause and move your head back. As you increase the "pinch" longer and longer you influence the person's breathing pattern. Her breathing slows down and the chemicals of calmness increase.

How do you know when to switch from listening to talking? When the person starts to repeat previously mentioned information you know that your permission (receptivity level) to speak has increased.

Refinement: Kinesthetic Method

So far we have covered the auditory and visual methods of influencing another person's breathing. The kinesthetic method involves respectfully touching the person in sync with her breathing.

As a learner

The Kinesthetic Method

Ask your partner to join you again. Have her sit in a chair while you stand behind her and off to her side. Rest your hand on her shoulder. Make sure you, at best, are only in her peripheral view. It's even better if she can't see you at all. Make sure you can see her breathing pattern.

Keep your hand on her shoulder during this whole process. As she inhales, you decrease your pressure or lighten the touch. As she exhales you increase the weight of your hand on her shoulder (avoid "clamping" your hand on her shoulder). As she again inhales you decrease the pressure of the touch. Do this decrease-increase several times. You have finished your pace; you have taken your cues from her.

Now you are ready to lead. This time as she comes to the end of her exhale, you hold the weight of your hand on her shoulder a pinch longer. This increases the release of chemicals of calmness.

Final Comment—Rapport

Pattern 17 addresses how to influence another person by affecting her breathing. The importance of knowing how to influence another person's breathing is best appreciated by comparing and contrasting how other models explain how to affect a person so that she will be more receptive to us.

17

Many methods of communication, notably Neuro Linguistic Programming, emphasize the importance of rapport. "Being in rapport" is described by such definitions as "both parties are comfortable" or "each party is able to enter the other person's world/perspective." Being in rapport is often achieved by matching/mirroring the other person's facial expressions, voice qualities and body posture. Once this rapport is achieved then the communicator can gracefully shape the other person toward some desired outcome. The matching/mirroring is referred to as *pacing* the person and the shaping as *leading* the person. Pentimento's focus on permission is advocating that:

- The NLP visual, auditory and kinesthetic pacing and leading techniques are attempts to ensure that there was cooperation between the parties.

- Breathing is a more sophisticated non-verbal than the visual (i.e., facial expressions), auditory (i.e., voice qualities) and kinesthetic (body postures) non-verbals.

- If the other person is breathing abdominal/low enough, there is no need for the visual, auditory, and kinesthetic pacing and leading.

- However, if the other person is not breathing abdominal/low enough, then the pace and lead skills are extremely helpful—but only in that the techniques lead the other person to abdominal/low breathing.

The Pentimento and NLP both agree that when the other person is breathing abdominal/low, her visual, auditory, and kinesthetic channels of receiving and processing information are open. Historically, the NLP techniques of pacing and leading the other person's visual, auditory and kinesthetic non-verbals were breakthroughs in communication. The Pentimento stands on the NLP shoulders and updates the NLP understanding by having the pacing and leading of breathing replace the pacing and leading of the visual, auditory and kinesthetic non-verbals. Since we have all been warmed by fires someone else has built, it will be interesting to see what will stand on Pentimento's shoulders.

Pattern 18. Pause, Breathe and Join

1-59

Effective oral communication includes not only the spoken content but also the pauses between bits of content. The question is, "Does the communicator join or not join the content that follows the pause with the content that preceded the pause?" Brain research provides the answer as to whether or not to join pieces of content. And whether or not the communicator is aware of the research, an effective communicator often knows intuitively when to join pieces of content/information and when to separate them. When the pieces of content are related, we want to join them together so that we can deliver more content. Simply, we achieve accelerated learning.

Pattern 18 delineates when and how to join pieces of content. Pattern 19 will address when and how to separate the pieces of content. By knowing how to use these two patterns we can be consciously competent because under pressure our intuition sometimes fails us.

18

Pausing sets up patterns 18 and 19. Pausing is usually done with a Frozen Hand Gesture. As mentioned on page 60, there are many benefits and uses of the pause. In this pattern, when we talk and then pause, the pause allows both us and our listeners to breathe. Because we and our listeners are breathing abdominally/lower, we all feel more relaxed and can think, speak, and listen better.

Why is it important to know when and how to join pieces of content? It's because the brain has a limited capacity to entertain new ideas. In fact, the brain can only handle between five to nine new bits of information at a time.[29]

$$(\_\_ \ \_\_ \ \_\_ \ \_\_ \ \_\_ \ / \ \_\_ \ \_\_ \ \_\_ \ \_\_)$$

If the communicator gives more bits of information than the listeners' brain can handle at a given moment, the listeners' brains become overloaded. Parts of the information drop out of consciousness—perhaps gone forever. There is a way, however, to increase the amount of information that listeners can retain and deal with.

Joining

If two pieces of content are related, connect them! That way, listeners will use up only one "slot" in the brain.

> ***Our goal is to connect related pieces of content together so that we can deliver more content and have the listeners retain more.***

The technique for doing this is deceptively simple: after delivering one piece of information, pause with a Frozen Hand Gesture. At the end of the pause, speak and move at precisely the same moment. That will hook the two pieces together into a single memory unit. By practicing and mastering the, "Pause, Breathe and Join" technique, we can help our listeners retain more of what we say.

For example, if a committee chair says, "In place of our usual interdepartmental meeting, we have a customer service trainer. Ms. Rapid Rapport will be talking about the change in our customer demographics." In this communication there are three messages:

1. "In place of our usual interdepartmental meeting,

2. we will have a customer service trainer.

3. Ms. Rapid Rapport will be talking about the change in our customer demographics."

The listeners could use the first three slots of their 5-9 slots of memory to store the information. Or they could occupy just the first slot thereby allowing them to receive more information:

In place... we have... Ms. Rapid... ___ ___ / ___ ___ ___ ___
    1   2   3   4 5   6 7 8 9

or

In place... we have... Ms.... ___ ___ ___ ___ / ___ ___ ___ ___
            1   2 3 4 5   6 7 8 9

When we pause [*hand gestures remain perfectly still*] after each chunk of information, our listeners hear the chunks better. And as we begin to talk again at exactly the same time as our hand gesture moves, the listeners unconsciously join all three pieces of the communication into one fact (with three parts) instead of three separate facts. One slot of memory is used instead of three. In reality, when we use the Pause, Breathe and Join process, listeners have just one bit of information to understand instead of several. They pay better attention, absorb more information and remember what they have heard longer.

18

When we pause by breathing without moving and then continue to talk, the information said after our pause is automatically joined with what we previously said. Here is a mnemonic aid: in the American culture a traditional sandwich is the **P**eanut **B**utter and **J**elly. It is very tacky and sticks to the roof of the mouth. So, too, the **P**ause, **B**reathe, and **J**oin technique sticks content pieces together.

The goal is to hold the gesture frozen during the pause. The Frozen Hand Gesture during the pause holds the listener's attention. In order for the speaker to freeze the gesture during the pause the speaker has to be gesturing while speaking. During the pause the communicator gets to decide whether to join (Pattern 18) or separate (Pattern 19) the content that follows the pause with the content that came before the pause.

If the communicator wants to join pieces of content (Pattern 18), then at the end of the pause he speaks and moves simultaneously.

If the communicator wants to separate pieces of content (Pattern 19), then at the end of the pause he moves silently and then speaks.

On the surface it seems that the stillness during the pause is limited to freezing the Frozen Hand Gesture and stopping the flow of words. However, the stillness applies to the entire body, specifically the head, eyes, lips and mouth. During the pause, keep the head, eyes, lips and mouth still. Then when "joining" have the head, eyes, lips, mouth and gestures simultaneously move as speaking is resumed. Having the body in perfect sync with the sounds coming from the mouth requires practice. Here are some guidelines based on communication styles:

- Auditory-oriented people tend to move their lips or raise their head before they start speaking. It is their way of getting ready to speak. Recommended solution: keep mouth closed and head still until the very moment the first word is spoken.

- Visual-oriented people tend to move their eyes before they start speaking. Recommended solution: practice speaking and moving the eyes precisely together.

- Kinesthetic-oriented people have a tendency to start their gestures before they speak. Recommended solution: practice speaking and beginning a gesture at the exact same moment. Even a nanosecond of movement before the words begin will diminish the listener's ability to connect what was said before the pause with the content said after the pause.

- For most of us it will take some practice to remain completely immobile during the pause and only start moving when our words come out. If our words and movement are not in sync it is better to have the words lead the movement. Our goal is to connect related pieces of content together so that we can deliver more content and have the listener retain more.

As a learner

18

Least Recommended Methods of Joining

With a partner do the following activity. Take turns as the speaker. When it is your turn say three or four sentences. Repeat these sentences three different times.

For each repetition intentionally do one of "Least Recommended" tendencies. That is, the first time do the
auditory tendencies of moving your lips or raising your
head before you start to speak. The second time, do
the visual tendency to change where your eyes are focused before you start to speak. The third time, do the
kinesthetic tendency to start your gestures before you
start to speak.

Debrief. If either of you has a slight tendency toward
one of the three "least recommended" styles—which
one might it be?

Recommended Way of Joining

Now do the recommended style. This time, stay still
during the pause. Have your head, lips, eyes, and gesture be in sync with your words; that is, do not move
head, lips, eyes or gesture until the precise moment
that words are spoken again.

Then discuss the experience of keeping head, lips, eyes
and gestures still during the pause. For each of you,
which recommended solution would be the most
promising way to improve your "in sync-ness?"

Pausing and Breathing

There is a second reason why the art of the pause requires
practice and it has to do with breathing. As mentioned
above, effective oral communication includes not only the
spoken content but also the pauses between bits of content. The speaker wants to breathe during each pause. The
inhalation usually occurs at the end of the pause. Actually
for many people it is better to start inhaling earlier during

the pause. By beginning to inhale earlier, your inhalation will be calmer, you avoid any possible gasping sound or inadvertent movement that otherwise might occur, and you can wait a moment at the end of your inhalation to get ready to synchronize your gesture and speaking.

In the example used to open this pattern a committee chair said, "In place of our usual interdepartmental meeting, we have a customer service trainer. Ms. Rapid Rapport will be talking about the change in our customers demographics." An effective communicator would pause after each phrase of the announcement and breathe.

"In place of our inter-departmental meeting...	Pause and Breathe Keep lips, eyes and gesture perfectly still until the next word is spoken.	we have a customer service trainer.	Pause and Breathe Keep lips, eyes and gesture perfectly still until the next word is spoken.	Ms. Rapid Rapport will be talking about the change in our customer demographics.

As the chair starts the pause she will hold her breath. At the end of the pause she will inhale as she prepares to resume speaking. The mechanics of inhalation encourages humans to move their head, shoulders and gestures up and back. This allows more oxygen to enter the lungs. While it is natural to move our head, shoulders and gestures during inhalation, we are more effective when we remain still during the pause.

18

As a learner

Inhalation at the End of the Pause

> Least Recommended: Practice doing the "least rec-
> ommended" style of inhalation. Sit with a Frozen Hand
> Gesture. Make sure the elbow, forearm and wrist are
> not touching or resting on the arm of a chair or a table.
> Close your eyes and be attentive to your inhalation
> and exhalation. Let your head, shoulders and gestures
> naturally rise up and back during your inhalation. Let
> your head, shoulders and gestures naturally come for-
> ward and lower during exhalation. Slowly open your
> eyes and watch as your Frozen Hand Gesture moves
> during the inhalation and exhalation.
>
> If you are practicing this activity with a partner, take
> turns having your eyes open and watching your part-
> ner with their eyes closed to notice how the natural
> expansion of the lungs affects the head, shoulders and
> gesture.
>
> Recommended: As natural as it is to move during the
> breathing cycle we want to train ourselves to remain
> still during the inhalation at the end of the pause, if
> for no other reason than we are indicating to the lis-
> tener we still have more to say. Practice remaining
> still while inhaling.[30]

Pattern 21 will explain how when we remain perfectly
still until the next words are spoken the listener sees us as
intelligent. In the Western culture when a communicator
does a movement from the other person back toward the
communicator, the listener unconsciously interprets that
the communicator is seeking/asking for something. This

means that when the communicator inadvertently moves his head, shoulders and gestures up and back during the inhalation at the end of the pause, he appears to be non-verbally inviting the other person to speak.

As a learner

"A Game of Interrupt"

- Sit with a partner and explain that we are going to play "a game of interrupt." You will say a message of at least 4-5 sentences. You will pause throughout the passage. You will begin each pause holding your breath and being completely still—head, shoulders and gesture. At the end of the pause do an inhalation and intentionally move your head, shoulders and gesture up and back.

- You have instructed your partner to try to interrupt you.

- Now do the same activity, only this time when you do your inhalation keep your head, shoulders and gesture still during the inhalation.

- Switch roles.

- Debrief and share the effects of movement vs. stillness during the inhalation. The statistical average is that the person tends not to talk when you are talking and during your stillness at the start of the pause. The person does tend to talk during your movement during the inhalation.

Final Thoughts on the Pause

As observers in a meeting or training we are able to notice not only the content being presented, but also the process by which the content is delivered. When we are in charge of a meeting or presenting a workshop our level of responsibility is much higher than when we are observers. When we are "in-charge" we cannot see the "process forest through the content trees." By pausing while chairing/ training we can start to approximate the ability we had as observers. Pauses are respites during which we switch, however briefly, from being content-oriented to being process-oriented… we notice how the group is receiving the content and, if needed, we can adjust style of delivery.

Various cultures interpret the pause and silence differently. For example, the Western culture has difficulty just standing still. Members of the WASP (i.e., White Anglo-Saxon Protestant) culture have the urge to do something. This is symbolized by the expression, "Don't just stand there— do something!" In contrast, members of the Eastern culture are oriented by the expression, "Don't just do something—stand there."

When a WASP sees a person who is still, the WASP interprets the situation as "the person is available." If the WASP needs to interact with the person, the WASP doesn't hesitate to approach the person. Yet if the person is moving, the WASP assumes the person is busy. The opposite is true for the Eastern culture. When they see a person who is still, they interpret that as "the person is occupied with thinking and is not to be disturbed."

1-60

Pattern 19. Break and Breathe

Pattern 18 outlined how effective oral communication is a series of "content" (spoken), pause, "content" (spoken), pause and offered a method of how to connect content that followed the pause with the content that was said before the pause.

Break and Breathe addresses those times when we want to disconnect two chunks of information. For example, we may have mentioned negative information before the pause and we don't want the negativity to contaminate what follows the pause. Another example is while chairing a meeting we had to manage a participant who was acting inappropriately. We don't want residue of the negativity from our management to carry over on to the content.

Break and Breathe allows us to disconnect two chunks of information or events. Simply, at the end of the pause, we silently move and then speak. Break and Breathe allows our listeners to continue breathing well and hear the content that follows the pause without getting distracted by what went on before the pause.

Break and Breathe can also be used to give listeners amnesia regarding any negative interruption that may have occurred. The secret to achieving amnesia about the negative content is to do each of the following steps with precision. Two variations are offered: the first variation is used for mild negative content.

1. We pause, completely stopping our presentation of content.

2. We move a half step away from that location. In the new location settle, then we speak about the mild negative content in a different voice.

3. When we finish speaking, we pause. In silence, we look down (one-point), breathe, step back to the location of the content. We continue in the

19

exact same voice we used before we mentioned the mildly negative topic.

If we have to communicate something that is very negative, we do the second variation. We do steps 1 through 3 in the same manner, then add a step 4.

4. Before we continue with the content, we settle (equal weight on both feet) and we exhale once more. Only after the extra exhalation do we speak, and we do so in the exact same voice we used before we mentioned the negative topic.

Vignette: Down by 12%

Paul Pausal knew that the board would not be happy hearing that revenue was down by 12%. Yet as the CFO he also knew that he was the best person to break the news to the board. Standing at the center flipchart he greeted them. Turning to the chart he outlined the agenda for the meeting. As he mentioned the fifth and last item he paused. Then looking down he turned toward a different flipchart, one that was off to the side. As he slowly walked toward the flipchart on the side, he held up his index finger gently saying, "Before we begin... ." The board hushed as he silently continued his walk. Once he arrived at the side flipchart he settled himself. As his eyes remained focused on the white paper, with great deliberation Paul flipped the blank sheet over the top and revealed the dreaded news. The chart, showing the 12% decrease produced gasps of disbelief. Paul remained silently looking at the chart as the stark reality settled in.

> As the group began to catch their breath, Paul, still looking at the chart, said in a very even voice, "We need to cover this concern." After an exaggerated pause, he continued, "And we will after we cover our five agenda items." He paused again. He stepped away from the chart, and while looking down he silently walked over to the original flipchart. Then he looked up and shifted to the quicker-paced voice that he had used when he greeted them.

As illustrated in the above vignette, Break and Breathe is often connected to Pattern 8 Decontamination. When a communicator is standing, the establishing of the non-verbals associated with two locations is blatant. When the communicator is seated, the non-verbals used for Break and Breathe are more subtle. When seated, non-verbals other than locations are used. If a communicator who is seated has been using a credible voice pattern and wants to switch to an approachable voice pattern, the communicator might want to Break and Breathe by just moving his head or torso.

Stress Management

Break and Breathe isn't limited to the concept of "decontamination." In fact, Break and Breathe is the Pentimento's number one stress management technique. The previous example focused on the communicator's interactions with another person. Break and Breathe can be used by the communicator to deal with stress not only in others, but also in himself. Break and Breathe is a Pentimento Pattern that separates the (negative) content that is said before the communicator's pause from the (positive) content that is said after the pause.

19

Since the breathing patterns are the most sophisticated of all patterns, it is only fitting that one of the breathing patterns deals with handling stress. Because of the importance of this pattern the following information is, of necessity, lengthy.

As a learner

Shallow vs. Abdominal Breathing

Pleasant thoughts are remembered with abdominal/ low breathing and unpleasant thoughts with shallow/ high breathing. This correlation applies to locations, tasks and people. To fully appreciate the importance of abdominal/low and shallow/high breathing, do the following activity.

- Place one hand on your abdominal area of breathing—just under the rib cage—and rest the other hand on your opposite shoulder. Think of a pleasant vacation. Which hand moved? If the lower one moved you were breathing abdominally; if the higher hand moved it is because the shoulders rose which indicates high breathing. Most likely when you reflected on the vacation the lower hand moved (unless of course you were remembering the bill).

- Now think of something that you don't enjoy doing; in fact, it is one of your least favorite responsibilities/chores/tasks. Which hand moved?

- Think of one of your favorite people in the world. Which hand moved?

- Then think of one of your least favorite people. Which hand moved?

- Then return to the favorite person and notice the fluidity of breathing.

As a learner

Inhalation vs. Exhalation

To appreciate the impact of inhalation and exhalation on the chemicals released do the following experiment with a partner.

Ask your partner to say the following requests to you. After each request your partner will be silent. Silently nod your head as soon as you begin to think of your answer to the request. No need to talk because the spoken content might distract your partner from observing. As you nod your head your partner will observe if you emphasize an inhalation or exhalation. The purpose of this activity is to notice breathing. It is not therapy. If the request accesses a major negative memory, shift your body and go on to the next request.

1. "Think of someone who irritates you."

2. "Think of one of your favorite vacations."

3. "Think of a social injustice."

4. "Think of one of your favorite food dishes."

5. "Think of an event that was disappointing."

6. "Think of an event that exceeded your expectations."

19

Switch roles and either use the same six requests or make up your own list. In the above list the odd numbered items were statistically negative and the even numbered items were statistically positive. If you try these questions on more than one person perhaps you will want to experiment and say all the negative items before saying the positive items (i.e., 1, 3, 5 before saying 2, 4, 6). Remember to end on one or more positive items.

Debrief and share if the recall of a negative item is accompanied by a high/flat inhalation and a recall of a pleasant item is accompanied by a low exhalation.

Updating Our Wiring

Without venturing into the area of evolution, suffice it to say that humans haven't updated their mind-body dynamics in the last 100 plus years. In the 1800s and before, one's survival often depended on the instantaneous release of the fight-or-flight chemicals. Even today, there are times when humans naturally want to be stronger and are wired to provide such a response. Watch when humans approach a heavy box that they need to move. Notice how they instinctively breathe in before lifting. Although such inhaling does make them stronger, they run the risk of physically injuring themselves.

There are two ways a human can injure his body. One is on the outside such as straining too much when lifting. The second is on the inside with the release of the chemicals that continues after he has finished moving a heavy object (a box). If a person injures himself by lifting (e.g., the back hurts) and he sets the box down, most likely he will continue to tighten his body to cope with the pain. The natural reaction is to grimace (breathe shallow/high) which incorrectly signals the body that there is still danger lurking and therefore more fight-or-flight chemicals are rushed to the area—exacerbating the situation. This natural internal response occurs even when nothing actually happens externally.

Think of the last time you narrowly escaped having an automobile accident. When you slammed on the brakes, even if you were externally safe, you may have had internal "injury." Chemically speaking, what the layperson calls "injury" has three parts:

1. Release of chemicals.

2. Internal injury due to the overload of the system = adrenaline rush. It is the equivalent of hooking a garden hose up to a fire hydrant.

3. Recovery from the internal injury.

As soon we are safe (e.g., the aftermath of a near auto accident), we want to stop the release of chemicals. We do this by quickly returning to full, deep abdominal breathing. Sometimes we have to be careful how we relate the story to others—we might reactivate the release of chemicals unless we remember to breathe well as we tell the story.

Vignette: Brother Thomas

My brother Thomas is 6′1″. I am 5′7″ stretched. I have one son 6′ and another son 5′9″. To make our family basketball games interesting, each team has a taller and a shorter player on each side. One

19

time we were playing a game while vacationing in San Diego. The blue skies provided the perfect backdrop in order to see the backboard. As the ball was shot from the outside everyone converged for the rebound. I could feel Thomas on my hip as we jumped. When we came down he wasn't in physical contact. By the time I turned to see what was the matter, he was already leaning against the fence with all his weight on one leg. We immediately stopped and gathered around him. He was breathing deep/low, emphasizing his exhale. Thomas said, "Sorry about the game. I've turned my ankle. I need ice." Within five minutes he was at the in-laws home with an ice pack on an elevated foot. Amazingly, he was walking the afternoon of the next day. Thomas is not only a superb athlete; he knows how to care for his body. When he twisted his ankle, he immediately breathed abdominally/low thereby signaling his body to stop releasing chemicals. The fewer chemicals released, the less likely the internal system will be overloaded and the shorter the recovery time.

As a learner

Rehearsing Convalescence

To help appreciate the importance of rewiring one's mind-body communication, stand up and pretend your left foot hurts. As you walk, inhale as you press down on your left foot releasing fight-or-flight chemicals. That is the innate way that humans cope when convalescing; however, it is ineffective to inhale at this time. It is exactly the opposite of what would be the healthy method.

Now walk and, as the left foot touches the floor, exhale.

We literally have to practice this rewiring. Those of us who might on occasion have a troublesome back/sciatic condition know that when the pain shoots down the back of the leg, the impulse is to breathe shallow/high. Instead, we want to practice breathing deep/low, emphasizing the exhalation. The next time someone is massaging you and the masseuse finds a tender spot, breathe out (Lamaze-like breathing)—the area will be more comfortable and you will be cooperating with your own treatment.

Along with childbirth and meditation, the world of fitness has been at the forefront in implementing breathing techniques. As recently as the 1970s, athletes were conditioning themselves by inhaling while exercising muscles. Inadvertently this maneuver caused injuries. With an understanding of how the body's chemicals change during the breathing cycle, personal trainers now instruct their clients to exhale during the straining part of the exercise. We have to activate relaxing chemicals when encountering physical challenges.

However, when it comes to the *strain* of interacting with another human being, we need, but don't have, personal trainers to remind us to emphasize the exhalation and activate chemicals of relaxation. While it may be injurious to breathe shallow/high when encountering physical danger, in some survival circumstances it is necessary to do so. But when communicating with people, there is no benefit in breathing shallow/high. Think of a verbal attack from someone. Although our first impulse is to breathe shallow/high—

19

we default to knee jerk reactions—what we really need in order to access our brain is the oxygen that comes with low breathing. High breathing is the innate response to being verbally attacked—we have to rewire our mind-body connection so that we breathe abdominal/low.

The following is a provocative example of what is humanly possible.[31] Chu King Hung, a Chinese Tai Chi master, maintains that one needs "paradox abdominal breathing" to activate the CHI, the mental energy. The master does a demonstration of four or five men pushing against him. With CHI and using only the tip of his index finger, he can repel the men, reeling them across the room where they crash against the wall. His theory is that animals have that breathing naturally but man lost it when rising to his feet and starting to walk upright. Zen masters also do this kind of breathing. How is it done? In paradox abdominal breathing your belly retracts when you breathe in and sticks out as you breathe out. When normal people are asked to do this they say "It's impossible." But when you cough you exhale and your belly comes out.

As previously mentioned Break and Breathe is Pentimento's number one stress management technique because it is a way to stop shallow/high breathing either by the communicator or the other person. An obvious question is, "Why not just label it Breathe instead of Break and Breathe?" The answer is best found experientially.

As a learner

The Function of the "Break"

Go back to the Inhalation vs. Exhalation section on page 155 and recall a person/chore/task you least like. As you reaccess the picture and the accompanying feelings notice if you start to breathe shallow/high. If so, keep your body in the same position and attempt to breathe abdominal/low. Memorize how much oxygen you were able to bring in.

Again recall a person/chore/task that is of equal negative importance. This time if you start to breathe shallow/high, break the pattern of sitting still by changing your body posture (i.e., move your torso; wiggle your body) as you shift to abdominal/low breathing. The break allows more oxygen to enter your lungs—hence the term Break and Breathe.

Application

Whenever you or other person stops breathing, the Break and Breathe technique quickly changes the situation so that both of you have more oxygen and thus more ability to think rationally. The most common time that the Break and Breathe is used is when doing Decontamination. In fact, Decontamination is almost impossible to do without Break and Breathe; in the land of Pentimento, they are the Siamese twins.

Recovery is More Important than Perfection

The concept of Break and Breathe is more than just a skill; it addresses a larger issue of professional development. Two avenues to professional improvement are:

- Plan and do.

- Do, review and revise. Reflect on what you did, then plan what to do better the next time. (Break and Breathe assists this avenue.)

19

Left-brained people are often perfectionists, very good at planning. They are attracted to the *Plan and Do* approach: plan carefully and then do it to perfection. In contrast, right-brained people are accustomed to making mistakes, to being less than perfect the first or second time. They are attracted to the *Review and Revise* approach: review what occurred and then plan how to do better next time.

There is an art to reviewing a situation that didn't work well. To get the most from a review, use a simple technique that involves changing pronouns combined with Break and Breathe. When reviewing the situation, use third person language to describe your own behavior; that is, instead of saying "*I* messed up," say "*The manager/consultant/trainer* messed up." That's the first step.

Secondly, after recalling what happened in third person language—as if you were a fly on the wall describing the actions of somebody else, shift your body posture (the "Break") and laugh heartily (the "Breathe"). Continuing to breathe well, *plan* the future by switching to first person. For example, "Next time *I* will…" or humorously, "Huh! *I* would never do what she did. What *I* would do is…" Reviewing with a third person pronoun removes guilt and allows for faster professional growth.

I propose a combination of "Plan and do" and "Review and revise." Practice the skills as if you are seeking perfection; yet, in reality whenever things don't go as planned, recover by doing a "Break and Breathe," then immediately change what you are doing.

Chapter Five

Special Pentimento Patterns

Overview

Although we list 21 patterns of non-verbal communication in four categories, there are only 19 distinct patterns. Patterns 20 and 21 are actually combinations of the other four categories but they are included because they are indispensable for effective communication. These last two patterns are great examples of the axiom, "What is truly effective are the little things we do. They are simple but not necessarily easy."

- Pattern 20, Voice Patterns and Breathing—unearths a great insight. People actually don't respond to the credible and approachable voice patterns (Patterns 4, 5 and 6). What they actually react to is the breathing patterns (especially Pattern 16) that accompany the voice patterns. Voice Patterns and Breathing explains the differences between being definitive vs. being angry and between seeking information and pleading for information.

- Pattern 21 Pause and Look Intelligent—describes one of our popular patterns. The pause is essential to the communicator appearing intelligent. No

---

To be respectful of gender equality and yet provide the reader with a fluid reading style, in this section the communicator is referred to by female pronouns and other people are referred to by male pronouns.

matter how intelligent we are inside, we still want to convey our inteligence externally. This pattern provides us with a way of letting our light shine outward. Pattern 21 draws from all of the four non-verbal categories of communication.

Pattern 20. Voice Patterns and Breathing

1-61~63

There is a misperception among amiable people that those of us who talk in a flat credible voice pattern are often upset. Likewise, those of us who are innately hierarchical, misinterpret people with a rhythmic approachable voice pattern as likely being doormats. It's not the voice pattern itself that causes the misunderstanding but rather the breathing pattern that underlies the credible and approachable voices. The following formulas are critical for changing this misunderstanding:

Voice	+	Breathing	=	Interpretation
credible	+	shallow/high	=	anger
credible	+	abdominal/low	=	definitiveness; sending info
approachable	+	shallow/high	=	pleading
approachable	+	abdominal/low	=	seeking information

These axioms are especially important for organizations. Because the higher positions tend to use credible voice patterns, there is a strong likelihood that subordinates will misinterpret the boss' intentions. Definitiveness is the intention of the superior, but if she breathes shallow/high, the employees think she is in a bad mood. Likewise an employee wants to be seen as cooperative, but if he breathes high, the boss thinks the employee is a pleading, spineless wimp. The breathing pattern, not the voice pattern, is the determining factor in how one is perceived by others.

Vignette: A Few Good Men (a movie)

There is a scene in the military movie where Tom Cruise has Jack Nicholson on the witness stand. Tom intentionally irritates Jack to the point that Nicholson's shouting shows spit coming out of his mouth. Most of us equate shouting with being out of control. Jack Nicholson is the consummate actor—he is breathing deep/low, not shallow/high, when saying, "You can't handle the truth!" He is emotionally in command of himself. He is yelling for the theatrical effect. The proof is how his face changes from indignant rage to complete shock by his suprise arrest.

I identify more with the approachable end of the voice pattern continuum and therefore have had to learn to employ the credible voice with abdominal/low breathing. One of the advantages of holding my arms parallel to the ground, which is what the effective credible voice pattern people do, is that I can monitor my breathing to be sure it is deep and low. Since my forearms are held at the waist, I can physically feel my stomach contract and expand as I exhale and inhale. So, while I would rather not shout like Jack Nicholson did, I do want to regulate my breathing to be deep/low whenever I am credible, especially when I am talking in a loud manner.

20

1-64~65

Pattern 21. Pause and Look Intelligent

The patterns of *pausing* and *looking intelligent* are closely connected. Why is this so? Simply stated, to be seen as intelligent in the Western European cultures, the communicator must have the ability to pause.

The Pause

Research indicates that non-verbal communication is more influential than verbal communication. Mark Twain was correct when he said, "No word was ever as effective as a rightly timed pause."

> ***The pause is the single most essential non-verbal signal.***

The following passage illustrates the universal importance of the pause.

Vignette: Verdi

Musicians know the power of the pause. Arthur Rubinstein was once asked by an ardent admirer, "How do you handle the notes as well as you do?"

The pianist answered, "I handle the notes no better than others, but the pause—ah! This is where the art resides."

Musicians even have a special symbol for the pause called a *fermata*. A fermata tells the performer to hold a note or rest longer than normal time; in other words, to pause at that point. But for how long? It's up to the musician, and this is where true artistry shows up. So when students ask, "How long should I pause?" there is no real answer. True artists pause until they feel it is time to break the tension created by the pause and that is entirely a matter of audience response and the musicians' own inner feelings.

Verdi in his most famous song from *Rigoletto* took this to the ultimate level. He stopped the whole orchestra for an entire measure right in the middle of the introduction. The audience was electrified by it the first time it was produced, and they still are today.

When you pause when speaking, you are seen as intelligent, confident and competent. Whether you are seen as a credible-oriented or approachable-oriented person, pausing increases others' perception of your intelligence.

The pause assists everyone. If you want to look intelligent, pause. This is especially important for the approachable-oriented people. How does the pause assist the credible-oriented people who are automatically seen as intelligent? They need assistance with not seeming stressed. When they pause they are seen as intelligent and more relaxed.

Look Intelligent

The three non-verbal ingredients of the pause are:

- *Visually*—be still
- *Auditory*—be silent
- *Kinesthetic*—freeze, weight on both feet, toes pointed ahead and, if talking, pause with a Frozen Hand Gesture.

21

Once the communicator pauses with a Frozen Hand Gesture, he then has choices. The most common choices are whether to then do a Pause, Breathe and Join or a Break and Breathe.

Breathe Through the Nose

As mentioned in Pause, Breathe and Join, effective oral communication is a series of speaking and pausing—"content (spoken)" pause, "content (spoken)" pause. Surprisingly, the communicator doesn't convey her intelligence during the speaking phase of communication. During the speaking phase it is her culture that is revealed. Her accent, speed of speaking, and style of gesturing all reveal her cultural influences. It is during the pause that a communicator conveys her intelligence and this phenomenon holds true cross-culturally.

Ideally, the communicator breathes through her nose during the pause while keeping her lips closed. Why? In the Western European cultures, a closed mouth is seen as more intelligent than an open mouth. Think of people sleeping on an airplane—one with her mouth open and one with her mouth closed. Which one looks more intelligent?

When Westerners watch TV footage of third world cultures speaking, the Western viewers do not see the speakers as intelligent because they have their mouths open during the pause. Understanding non-verbal communication is a necessary step toward removing cross-cultural prejudice.

When the communicator pauses longer she is perceived as more intelligent and more credible. In contrast, when the communicator pauses a shorter length of time others see her as less intelligent and more approachable. Both credible and approachable people need to pause. Why?

As the following vignette demonstrates, the pause not only lets the communicator seem intelligent, but also the listener.

Vignette: Credit Card

The power of the pause is usually associated with being the speaker being intelligent. A study by a major credit card company revealed that the best collection agents were ones who introduced themselves as, "Hello, my name is _____ I am calling from ___," and then paused. With these agents, customers very often would immediately say, "Oh I know I am late … I will mail it today." In contrast, the collection agents who didn't pause after they said the same message, "Hello, my name is ___ I am calling from ____ about your late payment …," found much more resistance and defensiveness. Apparently, by pausing, the better agents allowed the customers to also show their intelligence.

21

1-66

Refinement: Size, Length and Familiarity

There are three variables of group dynamics, each of which affects the length of the pause and the degree of amplification of non-verbal behaviors such as the Frozen Hand Gesture. Knowing how long to pause and how obvious to make the gestures is a key to being perceived as intelligent by a group.

	Pause Longer When	Pause Shorter When
Size of group	larger	smaller
Length of time together	shorter	longer
Familiarity of participants with one another	lower degree	higher degree

Patterns of Pentimento Summary

Visual

1. Points of Focus
2. Transitions Between Points of Focus
3. Peripheral Sight

Auditory

4. Voice Patterns: Credibility and Approachability
5. Voice Speed and Volume
6. ABOVE (Pause) Whisper

Kinesthetic

7. Physical Presence
8. Decontamination
9. Frozen Hand Gesture
10. Gesturing: Four Quadrants
11. Gesturing: Assigning Attributes
12. Gestures of Relationship
13. High Expectations
14. Kinesthetic Equivalents of Credibility and Approachability

Breathing

15. BLIP (Breathing Level Indicates Permission)
16. Indicators of Breathing
17. Influencing Another's Breathing
18. Pause, Breathe and Join
19. Break and Breathe

Special Pentimento Patterns

20. Voice Patterns and Breathing
21. Pause and Look Intelligent

Notes

Part Two:

How Not to Get Shot!

Chapter 6
How Not to Get Shot!

Application

This chapter is designed as a stand-alone. All the concepts from the Pentimento are explained instead of presumed. For the reader who has read the Pentimento, this design will reinforce your learning.

Overview

One of the most common situations we find ourselves in is having to deliver news that is other than positive. At best, it is precarious to be the bearer of such tidings. The danger involved is legendary. Sophocles, in his play, *Oedipus Rex* says, "Nobody likes the man who brings bad news." It is purported that the Romans, on hearing bad news, took their frustrations out on the messenger by killing him; hence, the phrase, "Don't shoot the messenger."

I took a managerial training that used the template of the *Four Temperaments*.[32] One of the suggestions was to have a sanguine (a person with the temperament of immediate, short-lived emotions) break bad news. Because the sanguine messenger would be more likely to empathize, he would be less likely to get shot.[33]

As messengers, how do we convey information that others may see as negative without becoming associated in their

---

To be respectful of gender equality and yet provide the reader with a fluid reading style, in this section the communicator is referred to by female pronouns and other people are referred to by male pronouns.

minds with the negative news? Our goal is to preserve the relationship while delivering the news. "How Not to Get Shot!" offers a way to do this through the eight components outlined in this chapter. Although the components will be examined separately, in reality they are interwoven to collectively create the fabric of "How Not to Get Shot!" The "How Not to Get Shot!" material comes from a bold vision created by Harvard University's Fisher and Ury. In their work, most notably *Getting to Yes,* they created the macro goal of preserving the relationship while grappling with tough issues. "How Not to Get Shot!" is the micro level of Fisher and Ury's macro model.

Component 1. Go Visual

2-1

When information is given orally, often the receiver needs the message repeated. Whether intentional or not, oral information results in the receiver depending on the communicator for information.

In contrast, information that is visually displayed allows the reader to look at the information as many times as necessary. In essence, visual information allows the reader to be autonomous.

Vignette: Reader Board

Before major airports had reader boards at the luggage carousels, people didn't know which conveyor belt would contain their belongings. The noise level was high and often people operated as herds, "Look honey, that intelligent-looking couple was on our flight. Let's follow them!" If there was an airline attendant present, that person would bark out the information with a voice pattern that most folks interpreted as "in-a-bad-

mood" or even angry. If you are culturally de-
prived of this yesteryear experience, just fly into
New York and clear customs. They still bark out
which lines are for United States citizens and
which are for visitors. Now with luggage reader
boards in most airports, the passengers are independent and autonomous. The atmosphere is
quiet and usually relaxed. Visual information less-
ens the noise.

Variable of Group Dynamics

When information is given to a group of people, the members will use a variety of speeds and styles as they assimi-
late the data. If the information is familiar to the listener
and if she is a quick thinker, then she will favor a messenger who talks quickly. Another listener who is not as familiar with the information and who processes more
slowly will want a messenger with a slower voice. This
same slow-talking messenger will irritate the quick thinker.
In a group setting it is difficult for the communicator's
speaking speed and all recipients' processing speed to
match. The faster processors misinterpret the slower
speaker as being less intelligent. Likewise, the faster
speaker misinterprets the slower processors as less intelligent. But of course speed of processing and intelligence
are two separate qualities. The beauty of going visual is
that people of varying speeds can progress at their individual speeds.

Speed isn't the only difference between people's processing styles. For example, auditory-oriented people actually
hear the information well, but often prefer to process by
repeating the information aloud at the expense of the other
listeners' time.

The group becomes split when information is presented orally. When the information is visually represented, people are able to operate at their individual speed and, in their individual style. The visually-oriented people see and the auditory-oriented people don't have to say it. Thus, visual information helps a group remain unified.

1

Vignette: The Ineffective Oral Meeting?

Frankie has called what was to be a short meeting to announce adjustments in work schedules with the pending summer vacations. As the manager, Frankie has tried to consider everyone's desires. However, the task is complex and Frankie knows that not everyone will be pleased with the changes.

Everyone is attentive when they hear the information for the first time. As they hear the information a second time, the members who comprehended the information the first time become perfunctorily present. However, when someone discovers that Pat's leave request has not been taken into account, the group realizes that the schedule needs to be modified. During the ensuing confusion, the manager asks for cooperation as everyone tries to understand how one person's adjustment has ramifications for others. Eventually some people's tensions increase, while those who are not affected by the changes begin to daydream. The group is definitely split.

Vignette: The Effective Visual Meeting

Ernest, having heard of the turmoil at Frankie's meeting, decides to approach his department differently. He passes out sheets with the pro-

> posed work schedule on them as well as having
> an enlarged copy attached to a portable white
> board. When an oversight is found, new propos-
> als can be visually represented for all to see. By
> doing so, the group as a whole understands how
> each proposal affects all members.

When listeners see information, their memory of the data is doubled compared to when the same information is presented only orally. Therefore, it is obvious that if something is important it is best to display or represent it visually. Not surprisingly, when we present information both orally and visually, the part that is visual conveys more importance than the part that is verbal. This is so universally true that in trainings and classrooms when the trainer or teacher switches from lecturing to showing data, the listeners increase their note taking.

Refinement: Visual Representation— Prerequisite to Thinking

Going visual with information is a prerequisite for thinking. The larger the group, the more information has to be visual for the members to think. If we define "thinking" as mental activities that involve extrapolating, evaluating, deciding, synthesizing and their related activities, we find that the prerequisite to these mental gymnastics is the ability to rearrange data and ideas. Only when information is visually represented can we rearrange it.

If you were asked to critique our National Anthem as to which are the two or three most important lines, what would you do? You would write out the Anthem, which is a conversion of oral memory into a visual representation. Only then can "thinking" begin. This truism holds even

1

in arenas that are usually thought to be associated with auditory processing. For example, Quincy Jones, the famous musical composer, sheepishly wonders if he holds the record in buying tablecloths at expensive restaurants. When he mentally hears a series of notes he immediately writes them down—this often happens when he is eating. What Quincy is doing is converting auditory creativity into visual storage because it is only then that he can rearrange it.

Visual representation is the prerequisite to thinking. Understanding this truism will prevent the bane of all meetings—looping. Looping is when information is repeated. And repeated. And repeated.

Vignette: Looping

The members of a cross departmental quality circle are present and in a good mood as they celebrate their first anniversary. Over the course of a year they have come to know each other as people. After the initial stage of discomfort, they have settled into sharing real concerns in genuine ways. At the same time certain members' pet perspectives have emerged and become part of the fabric of the group. As the festivities of cake and coffee finish, they collectively start to focus on the suggested topic. Tom, from Customer Service, starts his standard tirade, one that everyone has previously memorized. Mark, from marketing, is hooked and pops in his mental cassette and retorts. Tom, of course, loops back to the start of his message and runs his tape again. Anne rolls her eyes and looks over at her friend Weggie Go-Again.

The previous example was with an established group of people who had already heard the loops before. The concept of looping holds true, but usually to a lesser extent, for groups that are only recently formed.

Vignette: Looping in a New Group

The second meeting of the task force has commenced. Within half an hour the group is starting to sink into the quicksand of looping. Rhonda Redundancy has already stated what she thought was the key insight. But Igor Ego, who thinks he is probably one of the smartest people he has ever met, has followed Rhonda's comments with his own harangue. Rhonda is concerned that the group will forget her wisdom, so she loops back and repeats her original suggestion; that, in turn, triggers Igor to loop also.

Vignette: Visual Meeting Decreases Looping

Angela de Mello is preparing for the upcoming meeting. She wants to proactively anticipate who the hiccups might come from. Angela is aware that Ron, from retail, will be attending. She giggles to herself as she remembers how his earned reputation of saying the same thing over and over once caused someone to change his name tag from "Ron from Retail" to "Ron from Retell."

External Edie will also be present. Her style of processing is best described as, "need to talk in order to think." Angela fondly thinks of her cousin Constance who openly admits to having the same style as Edie—constantly talking. In fact, Constance bought herself a T-shirt which said on the front, "I know I am talking" and on the back, "And I cannot stop." Since most of the task force members are more visually oriented than Ron and Edie, they often are frustrated with the "talking twosome." Now Angie knows that Ron and Edie have valuable information that the other members would profit from hearing. The question is, "How can I shape their behavior so that their ideas are heard?"

Angela opens the meeting with, "Thank you for coming. Our purpose is to examine the environmental impact and acceptance by the community of some of our company's recent decisions. We want to keep in mind that, as a company [*Angela looks and points to the chart where one of Ron's infamous quotes is written* out: 'Without retail we would derail.' *She pauses, then turns back to the group.*] we wouldn't exist without our retail department."

As the meeting progresses, Edie speaks in order to think. Angela immediately starts to record Edie's thoughts on the board.

Five minutes later, Edie starts to talk again. As some of the members quickly recognize that Edie is repeating what she has previously said, Angela gently says in an intonation that curls up, "Is what you are saying any different than this [*Angela points to the written representation of Edie's original thought*]?" Edie stops talking and reads the written information. During the ensuing silence, the other members sit up straighter and are attentively curious. Edie has finished reading and, with her thoughts gathered, says some brand new information. The group is impressed with Edie's succinctness.

In reflection

Our ability to reflect is key to our professional development. In the above example it took several successful meetings, for Angela to recognize the strategies that made the meeting so successful. The first strategy was having Ron's thoughts visually represented because seeing his ideas satisfied him. Angela had proactively done this. Secondly, Angela's ability to recognize reactively when Edie was starting to loop and point to the board switched Edie's processing style.

In essence, Angela shaped Ron and Edie's behaviors from their innately auditory-oriented style into a more visual-oriented style. As a result, the group was both more cohesive and productive.

Summary

- Making a visual representation of volatile information is the basis for "How Not to Get Shot!" Most of the other components can only be implemented if *Go Visual* occurs.

- The benefits of going visual are many:

  - Produces more independent and autonomous learners with longer term memories.

  - Results in a more united group.

  - Provides the prerequisite for thinking.

  - Prevents or decreases looping; thus making meetings more efficient.

  - Provides the opportunity for proactive acknowledging.

Component 2. Get the Information Off to the Side

2-2

Once we have the information visually displayed, it is beneficial to get the information off to the side. Since our goal is to separate the message from us as the messenger, what better way to do this than physically? If we hold the information in front of us (on a piece of paper for example) as the listeners look at us, the message is literally directly in line with us. By holding the visual representation of the information off to the side, our separation from the bad news is more complete.

A quick review of "Points of Focus" will help stabilize this concept:

- Two-point communication is when there is eye contact between ourselves and the listener, termed as such because there are only two parties involved. This is the relationship level of the communication.

- Three-point communication is when there is a third point that is looked at by ourselves and the listener; this third point is a visual representation of the information. This is the issue level of the communication.[34]

If the news is positive, then a two-point (eye contact) conversation is highly recommended because the listener associates the good news with us. Conversely, if the information is negative, a three-point (get it off to the side) communication is recommended because it preserves our relationship with the listener.

Least Recommended: Second Point

Vignette: Participant Initiates Bad News

Robert Reuls has opened the meeting with all seven departmental representatives present: "Thank you for coming. Our purpose is to examine last quarter's revenue, compare it with the previous year's same quarter earnings and determine the variables that may have caused the fluctuation we are experiencing." Bella Cose from the Aggressive Growth Division, upon hearing the focus of the gathering is on the "variables," immediately bursts forth with a stressful sentence, "I think we should emphasize the company's expansion into the new markets that I have identified!"

Robert, using Rogerian empathy, leans forward and, with the soothing gentleness of eye contact, softly says, "Bella, we all know how hard you have worked on gathering the research information of the presupposed new cities. Sorry, this meeting is about the variables."

Depending on the day, Bella's reactions could be:

"No! We need to look at the expansion!"

or she could internally be thinking, "He is always so sweet. He has put me in a bind again. If I further object the others may see me as 'the brute'." Either way, by orally breaking bad news, she exacerbates the situation.

Recommended: Third Point

Let's contrast this same meeting with Robert using the three-point technique. Robert opens the meeting with the same verbiage but the non-verbal aspects are different.

2

(Vignette continues)

Robert, "Thank you for coming [*making eye contact with all seven representatives*]. [*Then, Robert looks down to separate the "greeting" from the content that follows the greeting.*] Our purpose is to examine [*turns toward a flip chart* (third-point) *and points to the first column*] last quarter's revenue, compare it with the previous year's [*pointing to the second column*] same quarter earnings and determine the variables [*points to a blank third column*] that may have caused the fluctuation we are experiencing." Bella Cose from the Aggressive Growth Division, hearing that the focus of the gathering is on the "variables," immediately bursts forth with a stressful sentence, "I think we should emphasize the company's expansion into the new markets that I have identified!!"

Robert [*turns toward the flip chart*] says in a calm voice, "I don't think so."

In essence, the flip chart (third point) has broken the bad news instead of the chairperson.

Variations

The above-recommended approach of using a third point is the skeleton. Each situation contains factors that warrant any number of modifications to flesh out the complete body of communication. Some possibilities might include:

When Bella was speaking, Robert could have listened with eye contact, leaned forward, made soft sounds and bobbed his head to indicate he was following (two-point) before he looked at the flip chart (third point).

Or Robert could have verbally identified with Bella (relationship) before switching to the flip chart (issue). For example, Robert, looking at Bella (two-point), says, "I personally agree that the possible long term solution might be to look at expansion; [*pause*] however, [*looking at the flip chart* three-point] the purpose of this meeting is ..."

Additionally, Robert could schedule a future meeting that would focus on expansion.

Group Dynamics Considerations

In the above example, Robert's recommended response to Bella is what might happen if Robert and Bella were the only ones present. How does the fact that this interaction occurs in a group setting make a difference? From a group dynamic standpoint the group's reaction to Bella's statement could influence how Robert wants to respond. If the group disagrees with Bella, then the above strategy works. If the group agrees with Bella, then she is the spokesperson for the group. If this is the case, the variables are so complex that a separate work is warranted. Our "Group Wizardry" and "Group Mastery" programs cover those variables and the options involved.[35]

For our present purposes we will focus on the former case where the group disagrees with Bella. Robert has two major considerations in mind when ideally selecting his responses:

- First, the rights of the individual versus the rights of the group

- And secondly, the methods of responding and the effects on the group dynamics

1. The epicenter of the earthquake of conflict is the rights of the parties. In one-on-one communication with only two individuals present, the rights of the individuals are paramount. This is especially true in our Western culture, with perhaps the 1970s being the recent high water mark. When we are in a group setting, we tend to behaviorally operate as if the rights of the individual are still paramount. The appropriate perspective is that the rights of the group take precedence over the rights of the individuals.

   The best blatant example of this is the innumerable times when all of us have sat through meetings where the chair, who is operating from the one-on-one template, is caught by one member. This participant has literally hooked the chair and is reeling in the attention. It is as if the rest of the group is invisible. Group reality stands still while the chair and only one member engage each other. It really doesn't matter if their conversation is intellectual, viciously attacking or tangential because all the other members' time and intelligence are not being respected.

One of the main purposes of our work is to offer a paradigm shift from being just one-on-one oriented to balancing the needs of the individuals with the needs of the group. This may surprise the reader who expected to read, "...to being more group-oriented." When we examine our society, we discover that we do contain subcultures that are group-oriented. One example is the military, where individual rights are subordinate to the group's needs.

2. On the surface, it seems that Robert, as the chairperson, is using the flip chart to manage the individual, Bella, hoping to increase her compliance. The reason we are seeking compliance from individuals like Bella is so that the group will perceive the situation—the individual is acting inappropriately. So from a group dynamic standpoint, the chairperson is managing the individual for one purpose only, and that is to improve the group's ability to function. If the individual doesn't comply, we still have accomplished our goal of communicating to the group that we see the situation the way the group does.

   Literally, if we manage for the sole outcome of gaining compliance from the individual, then we fall prey to operating from power. Instead we want to operate from influence. The power template is short-term, focuses on the issue level of the communication and is result-oriented. If the person-in-charge is power-oriented and the individual doesn't comply, more than likely he will increase his use of power. Influence is longer term, focuses on the relationship level of the communication and is more process-oriented.

Contrast this with the person who is influence-oriented and will not focus on the individual but rather on the group's response to the individual.

Least Recommended: Two-point

Vignette: Speaker Initiates Bad News

2

Candidly, Carl faces his company's employees for the annual "state of the company" meeting. Because of the need to keep their operators available to serve their client base, he will address half the employees at this morning meeting. He reports on the health of the company and announces that if the current downswing continues, there will be a 10% downsizing within the next three months. Carl then lays out a plan to rectify the situation.

In reflection

While Carl's intention was to be honest and forthright, the audience's anxiety upon hearing about the 10% downsizing resulted in their holding their breath while looking directly at Carl. This means that, unconsciously for sure, and quite likely consciously, the listeners now associate Carl with the bad news.

Recommended: Three-point

(Vignette continues)

During lunch Carl's intentions for the afternoon meeting remain the same and yet he reflects on how he can deliver the bad news better for the second meeting. Carl doesn't like how the morning audience went into a defeatist mental state. At 1:00 p.m., standing front and center, Carl begins with lots of eye contact (two-point), "Thank you for coming." As Carl pauses and breathes deeply the audience does likewise. "For our" [*using a hand gesture that went goes back and forth between the group and himself*] "annual 'state of the company' meeting, the following chart" [*Carl points and looks toward the left side of the front of the room*] "has been prepared." Silently he walks over to the flip chart. As he reveals the first column on the chart [*three-point: looking at the chart*] which shows last year's earnings for the same quarter, he again pauses and breathes deeply. The group also breathes deeply. "Let's look at what this year's same quarter revenues are." As expected, the members hold their breath as they see a decrease of 10%. It isn't natural, but Carl forces himself to continue looking at the chart (three-point). While still looking at the chart Carl says in a hushed voice, "If we don't turn this trend around within a quarter, there will be a 10% downsizing." Carl is pleased because the audience is still looking at the chart as he says the "heavy line."

He freezes for five seconds to let the severity of the thought sink in and to wait for the group to no longer be able to hold their breath. Just as they finally start to breathe, he walks back to the front center. Looking softly at the employees, he whispers, "And let's look at some of the things we can do about" [*mid way through the gesture of relationship he turns toward the chart and, with a vehement gesture continued in a loud voice*] "T H A T !" Carefully he turned back toward the group and in a confident voice prescribes a plan to rectify the situation.

In reflection

While Carl knew he didn't have the strategy of three-point on a habitual level, he was glad he had been trained to let a third point, in this case a chart, break the bad news. Carl could tell that the second group's optimistic expectation that the plan might work was considerably higher than it was in the morning session; it was as if the group had separated the bad news from him. Now he could be the harbinger of the solution.

Summary

- "How Not to Get Shot!" is the micro level of Fisher and Ury's macro concept of *Getting to Yes* communication. Fisher and Ury postulate that the three different levels of communication are issues, motivation, and relationship. The ones we focused on were issues and relationship.

- *Get the Information Off to the Side* allows for three-point conversations.

- The third point—visual display of the volatile information off to the side—can:

  - Be the source of management, thus preserving the relationship between the person-in-charge and participants.

  - Allow the chairperson to non-verbally validate the group's perception of an individual who is seen as inappropriate.

  - Foster a shift from individual rights to rights of the group.

  - Provide the chairperson the opportunity to operate from influence instead of power.

  - Separate the bad news from the rest of the information.

2-3

Component 3. Remember that the Listener Follows the Speaker's Eyes

In the previous example when Carl walked over to the chart there were several non-verbal components he could use. He could look at the group (visual two-point) or at the chart (visual three-point) while either gesturing toward the group (kinesthetic two-point) or pointing to the chart (kinesthetic three-point). In deciding what to do, Carl remembers that the listeners will follow our visual cues more than our kinesthetic cues. To experience this truism, try the following:

As a learner

People Follow Our Eyes

Show a person something on a piece of paper. Hold the paper off to the side to create the possibility of a three-point conversation. Look at person (two-point) and talk about the content on the sheet. (For instance, you might say, "Thank you for taking time to meet with me. I want to show you something that you might be interested in.") Alternate between looking at the paper and looking at the person.

Most likely the person looks at you when you look at the listener and then when you look at the paper, the person follows your eyes to the paper.

For most situations, where the speaker's eyes look (visual non-verbals) is more influential than where the speaker points/gestures (kinesthetic non-verbals). Simply, listeners follow the speaker's eyes rather than the speaker's hand gestures. This axiom is as true in a group context as it is in one-on-one situations.

To verify this principle, try an experiment the next time you are presenting to a group. Stand next to the board/ flip chart, point to the agenda and say, "Look up here..." Continue to look at the audience. While tapping the flip chart with your hand, say, "This is important information." You will likely find that the listeners follow your eyes more than your hand.

Refinement: Eye and Hand Coordination

While it is obvious that our visual non-verbals are more influential than our kinesthetic non-verbals, the coordination between our eyes and hands is powerful because eye and hand reinforce each other. When visual and kinesthetic non-verbals are perfectly in sync, the communicator seems natural and believable. The reverse is also true; on a subliminal level, the lack of coordination between eyes and hands can make a communicator appear incongruent and less professional. At worst, the communicator can seem amateurish and insincere.

As a learner

Being Out of Sync

Practice the previous one-on-one activity again with a piece of paper. To see if your eyes and hands are out of sync, hold the paper with your hand farther from your torso. This time when you switch from looking at the person (two-point) to looking at the paper (three-point), use your free hand (the one closer to the other person) to encourage the person to look at the paper.

The coordination between the eyes and hand when transitioning two-point to three-point seems simple. A closer examination reveals that most of us will switch one of our non-verbals before we switch the other non-verbal. For example, the hand may switch to the third point before the eyes move there. For effective communication eyes and hands should move exactly in sync. While our goal is to have our eyes and hands move to the third point exactly in sync, we may not be doing so.

As a learner

Verifying

Form groups of three. Have two people do the above one-on-one activity with a piece of paper while the third person observes. Talking and leading the listener to the third point, the observer notices if they tend to have their eye and hand coordination a bit out of sync.

The secret to coordinating the hand with the eyes is to look at the hand when switching from looking at the listener (two-point) to looking at the paper (third point). This is the focus of the next exercise.

As a learner

Coordinating both Eyes and Hand

Look at the person and say, "Thank you for taking time to meet with me. I want to show you something that you might be interested in." Simultaneously bring your free hand up so that the hand is directly between your face and the listener's face. As you start to shift your eyes from the person to the third point, look directly at your fingers. In this manner your eyes and hand are coordinated as they simultaneously shift to the paper.

In reality, it will be impolite to look at your hand when facing the listener. You were just putting your hand directly between your face and the other person's face for practice. As inappropriate as it is, looking directly at your fingers does help you achieve the coordination. Practice the previous exercise several times before going on to the next exercise.

As a learner

Peripherally Look at Fingers

Look at the person and say, "Thank you for taking time to meet with me. I want to show you something that you might be interested in." Simultaneously bring your free hand up so that the hand is below the direct line between your face and the listener's face. Make sure you can peripherally see your fingers. As you start to shift your eyes from the person to the third point, peripherally keep looking at your fingers. In this manner your eyes and hand are coordinated as they simultaneously shift to the paper and, at the same time, you are polite.

Both our eyes and hand gesture influence our listener. We don't want to split their focus by having either our eye or hand gesture be at the second point while we are moving to the third-point. Coordinating our eyes and hand when transitioning from a two-point to a third-point will influence our listener to follow us to the third-point.

Refinement: Two-hand Gesturing

In a group setting it is actually easier to do the eye and hand coordination than when doing the technique in a one-on-one setting because the group is farther away from us and cannot easily see that we are peripherally looking at our fingers.

Sometimes we find ourselves looking at the flip chart but don't know whether the group is following. How do we observe the group without disturbing the focus on the flip chart? The answer is to use two hands when gesturing. The next exercise explains how to do this.[36]

As a learner

Two-hand Practice

> Stand next to a real or pretend flip chart. Begin by pointing with the hand closer to the chart (kinesthetic three-point) while looking (visual three-point) at the information. Keep the extended hand where it is and turn your head toward the real or pretend audience. Extend your free hand (the one away from the chart) toward the listeners as you say, "So the next point we want to cover...." Turn your eyes and move your free hand from the group back to the chart.

This coordination of the eyes and two hands influences the group to direct their attention to the chart. As previously mentioned, coordinating our eyes and hand when transitioning from a two-point to a third point will influence our listeners to turn their attention to the third point.

Refinement: Peripherally Seeing

There is a major difference between one-on-one and group communication. One-on-one communication provides us with the opportunity to observe the other person because two-point communication is the norm. In a group setting, three-point communication is often the norm, such as when we are looking at a flip chart (third point). We have to create opportunities to observe the group.

How do we read a group when we are not looking at them, but instead all of us are looking at a third point? We pause. And we do so in a way that keeps their attention on the content and also allows us to look back at the audience. One method is to use a transitional preface, such as, "So the next point we want to cover is..." Phrases like this create an opportunity to switch momentarily from a three-point to a two-point focus, thereby giving us a subtle way to quickly read the group. If we turn completely away from looking at the third point back to the second point, the group will tend to look at us rather than at the chart. Therefore, we want to turn toward the group only as far as is necessary to read the group. If we stop turning toward the group as soon as we can peripherally read them, they will continue to look at the chart.

Refinement: Pause

The pause is the most essential non-verbal technique to master. There are two reasons for this.

- The pause provides us time to breathe more deeply, thereby allowing us to think better. When talking, we are exhaling. Why is this significant? When we are not talking we have an opportunity to inhale. The part of our anatomy that separates us from other animals is our brain. More correctly stated, "When we use our brain, we separate ourselves from other animals." We are most effective when we get plenty of oxygen into our brains. That three pounds of gray matter is an oxygen hog. The brain requires between 25-37% of all the oxygen taken in. Since the brain is so dependent on oxygen, there is a direct correlation between the amount of air taken in and our ability to think. Consequently, pausing allows us to breathe deeper—and think better.

- The pause gives us time to read the group. When we are talking, we tend to be mentally involved with content. For example, we think, "What am I going to say next?" Yet we know that the more we are attentive to the process of delivering the content, the more effective we will be. During the pause we have a natural opportunity to read the group; for any presenter the ability to read the audience is of crucial importance.

To keep the listener's full attention during the pause, a Frozen Hand Gesture is recommended. The frozen hand occupies the group's attention during the pause much like our words occupy the group's attention when we are speaking.

A simple, but not easy, formula is:

> *Pause + Frozen Hand Gesture = time to breathe and a chance to read the group.*

Exceptions to Eye and Hand Coordination

In general, we want to have our eyes and hand gesture coordinated so that we look and point in the same direction. The exception is when we manage. In the earlier section (*Go Visual*) Angela de Mello chaired a meeting. She was managing two participants who were loopers: Ron, a storyteller, and Edie, an external auditory processor.

3

Angela was successful in getting these oral-oriented people to use a visual processing style by systematically using her non-verbals in the following manner.

Angela Managing Ron:

Angela begins by saying, "We [*scanning the group and making eye contact with everyone except Ron*] want to keep in mind that, as a company... [*Angela points to the chart where one of Ron's infamous quotes, 'Without retail we would derail.'*] we would not exist without our retail department." As Ron hears and sees his insight spotlighted, he immediately drops his chin as his mouth opens and readies himself to talk. Angela proactively anticipates that Ron will want to speak as she says, "As we examine our company's stand on environmental issues...." She flips the first page of the flip chart and reveals the three major focuses for discussion. At the same time, without looking at Ron, Angela extends her hand in a gentle traffic cop "stop" gesture toward Ron. Ron closes his mouth and the meeting flows into an examination of the first item on the agenda.

Angela has opened the meeting with a verbal recognition to Ron and simultaneously non-verbally managed him. Angela is operating from the group dynamic template:

The group comes first.

Angela was able to do this by selectively looking at everyone except the person she was talking about—Ron. She was also systematic in doing a mild reprimand [*the "stop" gesture toward him, which is a kinesthetic two-point*] while she was looking at the flip chart.

Angela Managing Edie:

As the meeting progresses, Edie speaks in order to think. Angela immediately starts to record Edie's thoughts on the board. Five minutes later Edie starts to repeat herself. Angela points (kinesthetic three-point) to the written representation of Edie's original thought. Angela looks at Edie (visual two-point), and gently says with an intonation that curls up, "Is what you are saying any different than" [*Angela switches and looks at the flipchart—visual third point.*] "this?" Edie stops talking and reads the written information. Because Angela is looking at the content of the flipchart Edie is more likely to focus on the content and Angela's question. As a result of Angela's maneuver, Edie formulates her thoughts during the silence.... When Edie does speak the group listens to Edie's new ideas. If Angela had looked at Edie when asking the potentially volatile question of, "Is what you are saying any different than this?" Edie, and more importantly the group, might very well have interpreted Angela's behavior as a reprimand.

By systematically using two and three points to communicate, Angela successfully managed Edie with influence instead of power.

Summary

- Our visual (where our eyes are looking) non-verbals are more influential than our kinesthetic (where our hand is pointing) non-verbals.

- When we are making a transition from a two-point to a three-point, coordinating our eyes with our hand increases our ability to have the listeners follow our eyes to the third point. When we are in a group setting we often use both hands.

- The pause creates opportunities for us to observe the group.

- The pause with a Frozen Hand Gesture holds the listeners' attention.

- We want to increase our peripheral viewing so that we can easily read the group even when we are at a third point.

- There are times when it is useful to separate where our eyes look from where we gesture or point.

- By systematically employing our non-verbals, we can preserve our personal relationship with those individual participants we manage while keeping the group cohesive.

2-4

Component 4. Use Third Person

When communicating about volatile issues, we want to preserve the relationship between the parties. One way to preserve relationships is to only use third person pronouns (he/she/it). When we use impersonal language when talking about the issue, it is easier on the emotions of the parties involved. So we say, "the report" instead of "your report." In contrast, if we use first person singular pronouns ("I," "me," "mine") and second person ("you," "your") pronouns, the parties tend to get defensive. Why is this so? It's because first and second person language seems more personal, and potentially more threatening to the listener. By avoiding first person ("I," "me," "mine") and second person ("you," "your"), we minimize the potential for defensive reactions and injury to the relationship between ourselves and the other person.

Vignette: The Teflon™ Presenter

As a veteran supply salesperson, Ben Hex has been in this situation before. He is sitting in a chair outside the conference room waiting for the purchasing committee to call him in. Ben is pleased with the proposal that had been forwarded to the committee ahead of time. It contained all the pertinent information. He especially likes how he had outlined the features/benefits of this product. While the reputation of Ben's company is outstanding, he is concerned that his competitors have submitted proposals priced below his, even though it is unlikely that Ben's competitors can actually meet the promised volume. Ben knows that the CEO, who at this moment is meeting with the purchasing committee, will not be giving him an opportunity to "present" his proposal. His presence is for the sole purpose of answering any questions that Mr. Stoic may deem necessary.

The door opens, a signal that Ben's turn on the agenda has arrived. Entering the room Ben sees a massive rectangular table. Then Ben notices that the CEO is sitting at the far head of the table flanked by two executives. As Ben slides into the chair at the opposite end of the large table, he successfully hides a smirk as he thinks to himself, "Given the subservient role I have, I wonder if this is why in carpentry the short end of the table is referred to as the 'butt' end!"

Since Ben doesn't know how the committee, and Mr. Stoic in particular, have responded to his proposal Ben is prepared to be flexible.

- In case the group doesn't like the proposal Ben is ready to use his Teflon™ approach. By using third person pronouns only, any negative association will not stick to him. Instead of saying "my proposal," he will be careful to say "THE proposal." Instead of "your requirements" he will say "THE requirements," etc. He knows that if he can just remember to use the third person, he can keep himself from becoming associated with unacceptable aspects of the proposal. He also knows that if he forgets and says "MY proposal," he runs the risk of seeming defensive. By using more neutral references such as in "the proposal," Ben will be able to position himself as a third party mediator who could objectively explain segments of the proposal.

- On the other hand, if the committee actually likes the proposal, Ben is ready to use first person pronouns and identify with it. He will feel free to say MY proposal and OUR proposal.

As Mr. Stoic begins his inquisition, Ben, as planned, responds in third person language. In time it becomes clear that the group is gathering information and in no way are their questions a reflection on how they will actually evaluate the proposal. When Mr. Stoic himself asks Ben to allow the committee to caucus alone, Ben returns to the chair outside the room. Within 10 minutes he is invited back in. Based on the slight smiles on their faces, Ben correctly assesses that they have accepted the proposal with one slight modification that had been agreed to earlier. Because of the group's receptivity Ben immediately switches to first and second pronouns, "*I* am glad *you* like *my* proposal."

Summary

- If the other party dislikes the information then as messengers use third person pronouns or neutral expressions. For example, instead of saying, "*my* proposal," say "*the* proposal."

- Possessiveness ("I" "my" "mine" and "you" "your") leads to defensiveness. Avoid using these pronouns until you are sure the information is seen as positive.

- If the other party likes the information, we are not in jeopardy of being shot so we use first or second person pronouns.

Component 5. Separate the Problem from the Solution

2-5

The central theme running throughout "How Not to Get Shot!" is preserving the relationship while grappling with difficult issues. *Get It Off to the Side* covered how we preserve the relationship by physically separating the problem from ourselves as messengers. Likewise we want to separate the problem from the solution. Why is this important? Even if the recipients of the bad news don't blame us as messengers, sometimes they get mentally, and more importantly, emotionally, stuck in the problem and don't focus enough on the solution. Fisher and Ury suggest that while problems can be created by either the content of the conflict (issue level of the communication) or by the people involved in the conflict (relationship level of the communication), the solutions are almost always found on the relationship level because humans execute the solution. Simply put, look at a third point when talking about the problem and look at the person when talking about the solution.

> ***Look at the third point when talking about the problem and make eye contact with the person when talking about the solution.***

By using separate locations for the problem and the solution, we create separate memories. We want to keep the memory of a problem from contaminating the solution. For proof that locations have memories, think about where each of us was on September 11th, or where each of us was when we heard that Princess Di had been killed in an auto accident. This is why people are so selective on where to go for their honeymoon—it will be a life-long memory. For the group to focus on the solution, they need to free themselves from the emotional mire of the problem. Then their optimism will be higher.

The concept of using non-verbals to *separate* the problem from the solution is a classic example of the title of this work in that once the concept is presented, what was formerly elusive becomes obvious. To illustrate this point three vignettes follow. The first vignette uses location to *separate*, the second shows what happens when we don't separate our professional from our home lives, and the last shows how a doctor helps the patient separate a disease from their own identity.

Vignette: Locations Have Memories

As a consultant Abigail Acumen does 80% of her trainings with in-house people. She determines where to hold her trainings based on the morale of the participants. If the company is doing well and the relationships among the people are strong and positive, Abigail holds the training on the company's grounds. She does this because "work" is positive for the employees.

If the morale of the group is other than high, Abigail negotiates with the company to conduct the training off premises. The company grounds are contaminated—work is not a positive experience. She wants to change the location of the training so that when the people come into a hotel conference room, they are entering an environment that is different from what they are used to. The change in the non-verbal surroundings shifts the participants' mental state.

One of Ms. Acumen's graduates, Ben Internal, uses the concept of *Locations Have Memories* for in-house projects. The concept of "separating locations" isn't limited to just separating the problem location from the solution location. Even if the company is doing well, Ben knows that when a project is started the enthusiasm is usually higher than it will be later. When a new marketing focus is called for, Ben assembles the key players off site. The freshness of the new conference room creates a better environment for the brainstorm than if the same meeting had been held in the company conference center. When Ben needs to have a check-in meeting, he schedules the same hotel conference room. Being in the original environment reactivates their initial energy and enthusiasm.

5

Vignette: Behavior vs. Intention

Blain U. Smith was ambitious and had moved up the corporate ladder quite rapidly. As his level of responsibilities increased, he became increasingly obsessed with productivity. In his early forties, he noticed that the next rungs of promotion had stopped appearing. At first he thought he was a living example of the unfortunate practice of "being promoted into incompetence." His frustration continued to mount.

In the next passage, Blain's context of "work" contaminates his context of "home."

It spilled over into the world of his family—an arena that he had always prided himself on keeping as a sanctuary from the pressures of work.

The incident that forced Blain to take stock occurred when he was playing mixed doubles tennis with his wife. At the critical moment of the contest, Charity missed an overhead shot that would have won the game and set. Blain's temper erupted as he blared, "Why did you do that?" The rest of the match was spent in awkward silence as the coordination between Blain and Charity disintegrated. The car drive home was filled with loud words and finger pointing. The next day Blain took a long walk to settle himself. Returning home he apologized to his wife. Moved by Blain's sincerity and vulnerability she softened. Charity emotionally reached out for her husband both to empathize and to explore what had caused him to change over the last few years. As a professional herself, Charity knew how the pressures of the job could get under someone's skin and yet she knew that Blain had plenty of self-awareness. In the past Blain had had the moxie to figure out what was needed to make necessary changes. Whatever the causes of his unrest, Charity knew it was deep seated.

The next passage shows how Blain's promotion inside the company has affected him in that he can no longer operate on a "personal" level. Now Blain is seen as a "position." The context of personal communication is very different than the context of positional communication.

Over the next few months, with Charity listening well and asking good questions, Blain realized he had fallen prey to the temptation of blaming people for mistakes and screw-ups. When he was at his previous lower level of responsibilities, his contact with people was more personal. When he chewed someone out, he conveyed as a person how disappointed he was in the employee. Now he didn't know them individually as well. And, more importantly, they didn't know him as a person. The person whom he called on the carpet just viewed him as someone who was using the power of his position.

5

In the last passage of the vignette we come to the most sophisticated of contexts—the difference between a person's external behaviors and the person's internal intentions.

Blain's outburst on the tennis court provided the grist for the mill of insight. He knew intellectually that Charity didn't mean to muff the overhead shot. At the same time he reacted with extreme disappointment. He resolved to separate the person's behavior from the intention behind the behavior. Although someone's behavior can be appropriate or inappropriate, a person's intention is always positive. So if Blaine was going to get on someone's case he wanted to acknowledge the subordinate's positive intention and, at the same time, give the person specific descriptions of her performance.

As previously mentioned, the concept of "locations have memory" can be broadened beyond the limited axiom of "separate the problem location from the solution location."

I have a dear friend who has difficulty being in hospitals. Because of one negative memory, he has inadvertently expanded this difficulty to the context of medicine in general. He and I laugh because his wife is a most competent nurse.

The next vignette shows how memories can be triggered not just by location but by any set of non-verbals or context.

Vignette: Hospital Rounds

The interns were elated because it was Dr. Carie's turn to do the hsopital rounds with them again. She was famous for her bedside manner. As was the tradition, there was a meeting before the interns went out on the wards to practice their latest lesson on empathy. The bulletin board indicated that this morning's focus was "Breaking Bad News." Dr. Carie had the interns pair up with one being the doctor and the other the patient. As she had the doctors turn to the patients, Dr. Carie reminded them of what they had previously learned: "Eye contact is two-point communication; looking at the chart and X-ray are three-point communication.

Least Recommended

Dr. Carie knew the importance of keeping the third point cleanly separated from the second point. She wanted the interns to experience how a patient responds emotionally to various doctors' behaviors. To drive home the point she had them do the least recommended maneuver, "All right, turn to your patient, look them directly in the eye and say, 'I hate to tell you this but you have disease X.'"

Dr. Carie then asked them to contrast that ineffective approach with the *recommended* method:

1. Take a deep breath. Then, in a relaxed manner, look directly at the patient and say, "You are doing fine.'"

2. Have your hand and eyes sweepingly gesture and look toward the entire wall where the X-ray will be placed and say, 'If we had enough room we could put X-rays of all of your body up there.'

5

3. Turn to the patient and, if appropriate, jocosely say, "And as far as we know they would look good."

4. "To save you money we have only one X-ray we want to look at today." Put the X-ray up and turn the screen light on, then gently say in a whisper, "The (mention an organ or body part) has the condition called _____." Patient, simulate reality by holding your breath. Doctor, pause and keep looking at the X-ray.

5. Peripherally watch the patient's breathing. When the patient finally breathes, turn to her and say, "And what we are going to do about" [*turn toward the X-ray and continue*] T H A T is…."

Dr. Carie then had the interns discuss the difference between breaking bad news in a two-point manner compared to giving the bad news in a three-point style. As the instructor she elicited from them the insight that when the doctor looks at the patient and says, "You have disease X." it is likely that the doctors are inadvertently programming the patient, at the least, to identify with X and, at the most, to have their identity be X. Dr. Carie finished with the following summary:

"It is obvious that we want to have the patient be fully a part of her own healing process. We do this by looking at the X-ray when talking about the problem and looking at the patient when talking about the solution. The question arises, 'How does the doctor make the transition between the two?' To find the answer, let's first do the least recommended way: doctors look and point toward the X-ray and say, 'You have disease X.' Now freeze your gesture and turn it toward the patient so that your gesture is pointing directly to the patient. What the doctor has done is only half right; the doctor created a separate location for the disease—that's good—but then she contaminated her relationship with the patient by transferring the non-verbals associated with the disease back to the patient. Doctor, you got it right at first, then spoiled it. Remember to separate the problem from the solution so that the patient is truly a part of her healing process."

Recommended

Dr. Carie distributes the following summary sheet:

The recommended method is called Decontamination (Pattern 8) and it involves several parts:

1. Doctors go back to the part of the scenario where the doctor is looking at the X-ray and has just finished saying, "The (mention an organ or body part) has the condition called _____."

2. The doctor is peripherally watching the patient who holds her breath upon hearing the bad news. The doctor is very still as if the doctor is also holding his breath.

3. It is important that the doctor freeze his hand gesture when pointing to the X-ray.

4. As the patient finally breathes, the doctor simultaneously shifts his body posture while dropping the hand gesture and taking a breath. [*The hand that had been pointing to the X-ray never points to the patient.*] In order to help us remember this technique, instead of calling it "shift and breathe," we use the alliteration of "break and breathe."

5

Dr. Carie has the interns discuss how the Break and Breathe technique allows the decontamination. Decontamination keeps the doctor from being associated with the bad news thereby increasing the doctor's ability to facilitate the patient's healing. At the same time, when the doctor non-verbally assigns the problem to the x-ray, this prevents the patient from over-identifying with the disease. She writes on the board:

Pause + Break and Breathe = Decontamination

Dr. Carie knows from her own experience that the intentions of the doctor might be admirable but they are for naught unless the doctor's non-verbal behaviors congruently support the doctor's outcomes.

Summary

Memory can be associated with any set of non-verbals or contexts, not just location.

- Separating the location of the problem from the location of the solution allows for separate memories of each. For example, when working with in-house people, if the morale isn't high, meet off the premises

- Establish a location of enthusiasm then use that location only when you want to reaccess the enthusiasm.

- Separating negative medical diagnosis from the conveyances plan will increase the patient's positive outlook for healing.

- Separating "work" from home allows us to recharge our batteries better.

- Separating the context of positional communication from personal communication encourages us to have different sets of skills for each context.

- Separating a person's inappropriate behavior from her positive intentions that generate those behaviors allows us to accept the person while holding the person's behaviors accountable. Acknowledge the person's motivation before attempting to modify her behaviors.

The component "Separating the Problem from the Solution" is based on the Pentimento Patterns 8, 9 and 18. When decontaminating two sets of location/set-of-non-verbals/contexts, pause (usually with a Frozen Hand Gesture) and then Break and Breathe.

Component 6. Use Voice Patterns Systematically

2-6

There are four categories of non-verbal communication. The previous components of "How Not to Get Shot!" have focused on three of the categories.

- Visual: Where to look with our eyes.

- Kinesthetic: What to do with our gestures and locations.

- Breathing: How to keep breathing abdominally deep.

This component stems from the auditory category. Pentimento Pattern 4 taught us that our voice patterns range from credible to approachable. When we use a flat voice that ends with an intonation that curls down, we sound credible. When our voice is rhythmic and ends by curling up, we sound approachable.

When delivering other-than-positive news, it is extremely helpful to use both voice patterns. The key is to use them systematically. The following axiom summarizes Component 6: Use the approachable style when seeking information and the credible when sending information.

The correlation of voice patterns with two and three-point communication is:

Correlations	Credible	Approachable
purpose	sending info	seeking info
points of focus	third point	second point
level of communication	issue	relationship

Vignette: Lines of Communication

As an executive team, they were professionally proud of their accomplishments—a steady 7% increase in volume for their third consecutive year. They were equally proud of how six months ago they had personally resolved to make their communication at meetings more humane by bringing in a consultant, Lou Loveridge. The two members who benefited the most from the training were Harold Huff and Vivian Vehemence. Initially they thought they were being advised to tone down their passionate stands on issues and decisions. But they quickly learned that Lou was suggesting ways for them to express their positions and still keep the lines of communication open.

It seemed so contrived the first few times the group practiced the new guidelines. Even Harold and Vivian laughed at themselves as they artificially looked at a third point when they raised their voices, then paused and did a Break and Breathe in a voice as they looked at the other members and said words that encouraged input. Harold, while looking at his proposed production schedule for the upcoming quarter, said in his normal harsh voice, "This is important. The supplies have to be purchased with at least a three-week lead time." He held his gesture as he finished and followed his pause with a shift of his body (dropping his hand to the table) while he breathed deeply. Then, in his best effort to whisper, he continued, "We all know that by doing this proposal our cash flow is severely limited." As he scanned the members who sat around the table, he asked in an approachable voice, "How do the rest of us see the situation? Maybe there are options that we haven't explored that will satisfy both our supply needs and our cash flow."

The correlation of voice patterns with two and three-point communication is: When Lou debriefed the team, Vivian was the first to understand how she often argued for the sake of arguing. Even though Harold espoused a desire to listen to others, Vivian and others couldn't fully believe him. It was only when he finally used his voice systematically to separate his position on the schedule (credible voice) from his expressed desire to listen to others' input (approachable voice) that others could actually hear his views and feel supported to speak about their own ideas. Harold said he had a similar experience— when he was the speaker he felt phony when separating locations by voice patterns. He just wanted to pound the table. It was only when he was on the receiving end that he realized how powerful and effective the Decontamination, and Break and Breathe concepts were and how voice patterns made them even more effective.

Summary

- There are four ingredients that make up all of non-verbal communication:

  - Visual—where we look

  - Kinesthetic—where we gesture and locate ourselves; body posture

  - Breathing—how we breathe

  - Auditory—how we use our voice

- The continuum of our voice patterns has credibility at one end and approachability at the other end. A credible voice works well when sending information, especially when combined with looking at the third point and focus on the *issue* level of communication. An approachable voice is best when seeking information, preferably with eye contact (second point) and emphasis on the *relationship*.

- By systematically using both voice patterns we can express vehemence and passion and still keep the lines of communication open.

2-7

7. Use Specific Descriptions; Avoid Interpretations

This is the most unusual of "How Not to Get Shot" components. It is most unusual in that the need for the skill doesn't arise very often. Yet when the need does arise, it is potentially the deadliest of all situations. Understanding and practicing this skill is equivalent to paying your monthly insurance premium—you "have it" although you hope you never have to use it.

In a conflict, when parties are able to stay with facts, the conversation is about sorting out what the facts are. Once one of the parties jumps from the facts, or a description of the facts, to a volatile interpretation of the facts, the likelihood of a peaceful resolution is very low. An example from our personal life will shed light on what happens at work. In conflicts in our personal life, the parties are likely to become heated more quickly than they do at work. Compared to conflicts at work, conflicts at home are more blatant. The following is a conversation between a teenager and her parents that has gone sour.

They are arguing about how late she can stay out. At some point the adolescent plays her trump card, and says with exasperation, "Don't you trust me?!"

Talking about "11:30 p.m." vs. "1:00 a.m. is a focus on facts. "Trust" is a interpretation.

Living with a teenager is an adventure in living with escape artist. An adolescent wants to escape from self-reflection and accountability. The teen does this by changing the focus from factual descriptions to interpretation. We have a seminar for bewildered parents of adolescents entitled, "U.F.O.", which stands for "Unidentifiable, Formerly Ours." When parents and a teenager clash, the entanglement might best expressed by the saying,

> *Arguing with an adolescent is a little like*
> *mud wrestling with a pig.*
> *Both of you get dirty but only one of you enjoys it.*

When she says, "Don't you trust me?" the folks are put into a reactive posture. If they say "Yes," the unlicensed adolescent attorney will quickly seek closure with, "Good! See ya."

If they say "No," the relationship level of the communication is questioned and damaged.

In an argument, whoever establishes the central question has an advantage. The teenager has initiated the focus on "trust." The first of many interpretative mud wrestling rounds. The parents'choices are now limited. Instead of reacting to their daughter's retort about "trust," the parents want to be proactive. They want to set the ground rules of what the discussion will be about (in this case, the specific time that she has to be home) instead of letting their daughter take the discussion into the realm of interpretation. The over-arching concern is this: how can the parents see the question of "trust" coming up *before* it surfaces. Instead of being reactive, the parents want to be proactive; they want to set the ground rules of what the discussion will be about.

When the parents suspect their daughter will broach an interpretative focus, they want to open by taking the "wind out of her sails." This is done by acknowledging her possible concern. A preface of "You may think that this is about whether we trust you. [*pause*] It isn't. That is not the question. The question is...."

The deadly vice of jumping from facts to interpretation is rampant in organizations. The proper words to describe when one group has a solidified interpretation toward another group are "prejudice" and "bias." Two examples of prejudicial words are "always..." and "never...." The next vignette illustrates the tendency toward prejudice and offers a method for breaking the stereotype.

Vignette: You Guys Always...

As Ingrid Introspect walked the short distance between her building that housed the accounting department to the newer structure for marketing, she reflected on how in the past these infrequent morning meetings were natural caffeine rushes with members of both departments implying that the other group was intentionally making their jobs harder. Both groups had negative interpretations of one another. She always knew that the meeting was beginning to deteriorate from specifics when people started accusing one another, saying, "You never ..." and "You guys always ... ." The classic posture of marketing was that accounting was stonewalling with forms and formalities that were irrelevant. Accounting retorted that marketing over-promised the clients without first checking to see if what was promised was financially feasible.

Bowling League?

7

Ingrid smiled as she walked, glad that those were memories of yesteryear. She was part of the joint committee that interviewed and hired Sam from Serendipity Solutions. They were impressed that Sam operated from the premise that people consistently chose to work in a humane environment rather than make more money under less pleasant work conditions. Sam knew if he could get the personnel from each department to know each other they would tend to move away from their negative interpretations. They would have the ability to see the facts as facts. The group had balked at his suggestion to move the departments into common quarters to increase the relationship level of contact.

So when the idea to move people in the same building didn't work, Sam switched from a direct to an indirect solution—a company sponsored bowling league. There was one condition: teams of four could have a maximum of two members from the same department. Committee members realized that what appeared to be a socio-recreational activity was really a *conspiracy of love*. As team members got to know each other away from the job, the trust level at work increased. This was as true for those who directly knew each other as it was for those who didn't. For example, if Sally from accounting was going over to see Eugene in engineering, Brian from accounting, who was on Eugene's team, would have Sally say "Hi" for him. At meetings, people who didn't know people from other departments automatically assigned "positive intention" to those present because someone from their department emotionally endorsed people from the other department. Committee meetings were really about processing specific data.

Sam had said, "Most of the time the solutions are human. We all have a 'victim' part of us that was formed when we were adolescents; this young victim part can be reactivated as adults. To prevent that from happening, we have to proactively change how people interact with one other."

Ingrid would enjoy this meeting. The members know each other personally and have formed an excellent functioning group so even if the meeting doesn't go smoothly she knows that the people will assign to each other positive intentions. The committee will be able to unemotionally grapple with differences over the facts.

Summary

- When one person says a negative interpretation, it is likely that the other person will respond in kind. The most common evidence that interpretations are being used is the appearance of, "You always..." and "You never..."

- It is more effective to proactively acknowledge the other party's possible interpretation than to wait for the negative interpretation and then react to it.

- The more volatile the situation the more important it is to remain factual and sensory specific.

Component 8. Position Your Body at 90°

2-8

8

This component is a kissing cousin to "Getting It Off to the Side." When we position ourselves across from the other person, we are automatically at a second point. When we are at a ninety-degree angle, the third point is a more natural part of the conversation. In some situations, however, side-by-side works as well or better than 90°.

Vignette: The BIG Table

Paul Pliant, from the plastic research and development department, is ushered in to sit and wait for Mr. Ardor to return from a meeting next door that is apparently running late. Paul had heard that Mr. Ador's high level office was famous but he never knew any specifics. But there it is occupying almost half of the 10' x 12' room—the table—it isn't just a desk. "Pretentious" first comes to mind, quickly followed by "gauche" and "why?" Such thoughts are quickly interrupted as Mr. Ardor enters the room. With a perfunctory handshake and a quick glance at his watch, Mr. Ardor sits behind the table directly across from Paul. Whether the table is intended to have that effect or not, Paul feels much smaller and less confident. He wonders why he has even volunteered to represent some of his colleagues' concerns about their immediate boss, Mr. Pale. Although Paul has rehearsed an opening statement, "Don't shoot me but I think you would like to know...," he just can't muster the courage to start his rehearsed script. Paul stumbles through five minutes of incoherent ramblings, gripping the prepared papers in his hand. The vertical furrows on Mr. Ardor's forehead are deepening as he sits on the edge of his chair.

Paul is smart enough to excuse himself for a restroom break. All the way to the restroom he berates himself, "Stupid! Stupid! What is wrong with you?" Once truly alone Paul gathers himself by breathing deeply and in so doing lowers his metabolism. As he reflects in a calmer state, he is stunned that the size of the table has affected him like it did. As he leaves the sanctuary of the bathroom, he doesn't know exactly what he is going to do but he does know it will be different from what he has done so far.

Second Chance:

As Paul reenters Mr. Ardor's office, Paul avoids the chair he had sat in earlier and intuitively selects the chair next to it. He instinctively places the papers he has in the former chair. Turning almost at a perpendicular angle between where Mr. Ardor is sitting and the contaminated chair, Paul begins with a clear voice, "That (pointing to the previous chair he sat in) didn't work. Let's start again. You may or may not be fully aware of the morale and productivity conditions within the plastic research and development department.

You may be asking yourself why I am meeting with you instead of voicing our concerns to our immediate boss. We have tried that without success. And as hackneyed as it sounds, it is out of loyalty to the company that I am approaching you directly—of course our reputation as a division is at stake. By sharing with you our concerns, you will know best what to do about it."

Mr. Ardor's forehead is smooth and he is sitting back in his chair breathing well. Paul is pleased with the clear and succinct preface. It is without interpretations of blame, just accurate descriptions. The rest of the meeting goes well. It is a classic example of Mr. Ardor's seeking information before entering the final phase of, "And what would you recommend?" Paul is surprised and honored by this question. Paul mentally noted that he wants to remember to be as professional and systematic as Mr. Ardor is.

Pleased with the interaction with a boss two levels above him, Paul floats back to his small cubicle. He chuckles as he notices how his desk is built into the divider/partition-wall. He thinks half aloud—it isn't *the table* itself but how it is set up to promote a two-point conversation. It is serendipitous that Paul had created a third point by using the contaminated chair—thus allowing him to operate at a 90° angle.

White Board

Most executive offices have a white board. When people are talking, inevitably one person walks over and writes data on the board. Often a *third point* is unintentionally created and the person scribing is likely to have posi-tioned her body at a 90° angle to the group.

In an earlier vignette (page 189) Carl had used a flip chart to communicate to a group. When he pointed out the bad information (i.e., a possible 10% downsizing), he didn't face the group, but instead he stood sideways at 90°.

Summary

- Positioning our body at 90° allows us to rotate between 2-point and 3-point communication.

- Once the third point is created then the rest of the components of "How Not to Get Shot!" fall into place better.

How Not to Get Shot! Summary

1. Go Visual
   This allows you to use a third point which is especially useful when dealing with volatile information.

2. Get the Information Off to the Side

3. Remember that the Listener Follows the Speaker's Eyes
   Look where you want your listeners to look.

4. Use Third Person
   For example, use pronouns he/she/it; the report...., the situation.... Avoid I, me, mine, you, your.

5. Separate the Problem from the Solution

6. Use Voice Patterns Systematically
   When looking at a third point, use a credible voice (flat voice pattern with final intonation curling down ⟍).

   When looking at a person, use an approachable voice (rhythmic voice pattern with final intonation curling up ∧∧⌣).

7. Use Specific Descriptions; Avoid Interpretations

8. Position Your Body at 90°
   This naturally leads to three-piont communication. In some situations, side-by-side works as well or better than 90°.

Notes

End Notes

1. (p. 3) Rene-Marc Mangin *Minds in Motion* (2006) p. 15; Albert Mehrabian 1972, Patrick Miller 1981, Dale Leathers (1992)

2. (p. 6) See page 7 "Note to the NLP Reader" for more details.

3. (p. 25) Susan Albert, Educational Coach for MGA.

4. (p. 25) The word "quintessential" has two roots: "quint" (meaning "five") and "essentia" (meaning "essence"). The ancient Greeks recognized four essential elements, fire, air, water, and earth. Likewise, *The Science of Non-Verbal Communication* is composed of four essential elements: the categories of visual, auditory, kinesthetic and breathing. The Pythagoreans added a fifth and called it nether, the fifth essence, which they said flew upward at creation and out of it the stars were made. So, too, by using the visual, auditory, kinesthetic, and breathing skills we rise above the science and achieve the stardom of permission, the communication world's fifth essence.

5. (p. 26) Alexander Christiani; personal communication. (Germany's leading motivational speaker and a graduate of Michael's programs)

6. (p. 47) Gray, John. (1992) *Men are from Mars, Women are from Venus*. New York: Harper Collins. Tannen, Deborah. (1990) *You Just Don't Understand*. New York: Ballantine Books.

7. (p. 53) Peter Senge, author of *The Fifth Discipline*.

8. (p. 55) Sources include Ned Hermann, *The Creative Brain*; John Gray, *Men are from Mars, Women are from Venus*; Deborah Tannen, *You Just Don't Understand*.

9. (p. 58) *The Fifth Discipline*.

10. (p. 61) Applying this concept of "public image when in public" to the classrooms' cultures of credibility and approachability, individual members from both groups may privately appreciate a teacher intervening with an individual who is disrupting the class, but only the credible culture encourages public display of the appreciation." Gottman, John *The Relationship Cure*, 2001, Crown Publishers, NY page 174

11. (p. 62) From Fisher and Ury's model of conflict. See page 16.

12. (p. 72) Naisbitt, John. *Megatrends: Ten New Directions Transforming Our Lives*.

13. (p. 76) See *ENVoY*, pages 62-65 Once he starts to exhale, the communicator can approach, looking at the work in front of the person.

14. (p. 101) Pattern 4 introduced the concept that effective oral con-versation is a series of "content" (spoken), pause, "content" (spoken), pause.

15. (p. 101) Patterns 18 through 21 will cover several other impressions.

16. (p. 103) First introduced on page 60.

17. (p. 104) More and more newscasters stand. Standing allows them to breathe lower resulting in their voice carrying better.

18. (p. 114) A famous anthropologist married to Gregory Bateson.

19. (p. 114) Stretton Smith's #4T Prosperity Program.

20. (p. 116) The breathing patterns explain why we want to follow our ABOVE (Pattern 6) with a whisper.

21. (p. 117) Diana Ackerman, *A Natural History of the Senses*, pages 6 and 7.

22. (p. 117) *Creative Syndicate*

23. (p. 123) Norman Cousins, *Anatomy of an Illness*; quoted in *The Oregonian*, 4 October 2006.

24. (p. 123) A reference to a series of books by Jack Canfield and Mark Victor Hansen that had the phrase "chicken soup" in the titles.

25. (p. 128) Gary Larsen, public presentation in Portland, Oregon.

26. (p. 134) *A Natural History*.

27. (p. 134) Eva Johansson, *Relaxation and Mental Training*.

28. (p. 138) As mentioned in the Introduction, this concept is referring to the fourth level of professional development. A few cautions are warranted. If you are unable to shift the person's rapid breathing cycle within a minute, then consider that the timing of when you changed from the "pace" to the "lead" may have been off. Consider pacing longer. Be careful because the longer you pace the other person, the more you are in jeopardy of being led by that person. Another caution: if you are unable to shift the person, then consider yourself "contaminated." Review Pattern 8. If you were able to shift the person's breathing, it may not have been that you actually "led" them as much as that you interrupted their rapid breathing pattern. It doesn't matter. You still achieved your outcome whether you led them or interrupted them.

29. (p. 142) "According to some new studies the brain has more limited capacity for immediate memory than previously thought." *Differentiation Through Learning Styles* and Memory, page 51. Marilee Sprenger.

30. (p. 148) Some people find it easier to stay still by inhaling before the end of the pause.

31. (p. 160) Rudolf Schulte-Pelkum, personal communication.

32. (p. 174) Galen, the Greek, started the whole *mess* of trying to understand personalities. We use the word *mess* because after people died he secretly cut them open to see if there was evidence of why the person had the temperament he/she did. The other three styles were: Choleric (initial strong reactions that last), Melancholy (initial weak reactions but steadfastly remain and grow), and Phlegmatic (no initial or long-lasting reactions). His evidence? The color of the person's bile. Now isn't this a fine example of learning more than you want to know!

33. (p. 174) For some reason a messenger's permission to empathize with the other person decreases when there is more than one person receiving the bad news. In group dynamics the messenger's permission to empathize with another person or the group in general is based on numerous variables. These are addressed in our separate programs just for group dynamics, "Group Wizardry" and 16-day "Group Mastery" certification training. See our website www.michaelgrinder.com for upcoming trainings.

34. (p. 183) Fisher, Ury and Patton.

35. (p. 186) Check website for details: www.michaelgrinder.com.

36. (p. 196) First introduced on page 39.

Bibliography

Ackerman, Diane. *A Natural History of the Senses*.

Canfield, Jack and Hanson, Mark Victor (2002). *Chicken Soup for the Soul*. Health Communications

Clancy, Tom (1987). *Patriot Games*. New York: Putnam.

Costa, Arthur L. & Garmston, Robert J. (2002). *Cognitive Coaching: A Foundation for Renaissance Schools*. Norwood, MA: Christopher-Gordon Publishers.

Cousins, Norman (1981). *Anatomy of an Illness as Perceived by the Patient*. Toronto: Bantam Books.

Covey, Stephen R. (1997). *Seven Habits of Highly Effective People*. New York: Simon & Schuster.

Ekman, Paul, (2003) *Emotions Revealed*. New York: Times Books.

Ekman, Paul and Friesen, Wallace V. (1972) Original Study.

Fisher, Roger, Patton, Bruce M., & Ury, William (1981). *Getting to Yes: Negotiating Agreement Without Giving in*. New York: Houghton Mifflin Company.

Fisher, Roger, & Brown, Scott (1988). *Getting Together—Building a Relationship that Gets to Yes*. New York: Houghton Mifflin Company.

Fisher, Roger, & Brown Scott (1989). *Getting Together—Building Relationships as we Negotiate*. New York: Penguin Books.

Fisher, Roger, & Sharp, Alan (1998). *Getting it Done—How to Lead When You're not in Charge*. New York: Harper Business.

234 • The Elusive Obvious

Frankl, Victor. (1959) *From Death Camp to Existentialism*. Boston: Beacon Press.

Gardner, Howard (1993). *Multiple Intelligences: The Theory in Practice*. New York: Basic Books.

Gray, John (1992). *Men are From Mars, Women are From Venus*. New York: Harper Collins.

Grinder, John and Bandler, Richard. *Frogs Into Princes*.

Harris, Thomas Anthony (1969). *I'm OK, You're OK—a Practical Guide to Transactional Analysis*. New York: Harper & Row.

Hermann, Ned (1988). *The Creative Brain*. Brain Books.

Johansson, Eva. *Relaxation and Mental Training for a Richly Fulfilled Life*, book and CD.

Larson, Gary (1982). *The Far Side*. Kansas City, MO: McMeel Publishing.

Leathers, Dale G. (1992). *Successful Nonverbal Communication: Principles and Applications* (2nd ed.). New York: Macmillan.

Mangin, Rene'-Marc (2006). *Minds in Motion*. Philadelphia: Xlibris.

McCann-Hamilton, Vivian (2007) *Human Relations* New Jersey: Prentice Hall

McLuhan, Marshall (1964). *Understanding Media: The Extensions of Man*. New York: McGraw-Hill.

Mehrabian, Albert (1972). *Nonverbal Communication*. Chicago: Aldine-Atherton.

Miller, George A. (1956). "The magical number seven, plus or minus two: Some limits on our capacity for processing information," In *Psychological Review*, Vol. 63.

Miller, Patrick (1981). *Nonverbal Communication.*
    "What research Says to the Teacher." Washing-
    ton, DC: National Education Association.

Naisbitt, John (1982). *Megatrends: Ten New Directions*
    Transforming Our Lives. New York: Warner.

O'Connor, Joseph, & Seymour, Jon (1990). *Introducing*
    Neuro Linguistic Programming. England:
    Thorsons.

Rogers, Carl (1961). *On Becoming a Person.* Boston:
    Houghton Mifflin.

Senge, Peter (1990). *The Fifth Discipline.* New York:
    Doubleday.

Sprenger, Marilee (2003). *Differentiation Through*
    Learning Styles and Memory. Corwin Press.

Tannen, Deborah (1990). *You Just Don't Understand.*
    (1995) *Talking from 9-5.* New York: William
    Morrow & Company.

Ury, William (1991). *Getting Past No: Negotiating With*
    Difficult People. New York: Bantam Books.

Index

The Elusive Obvious—The Science of Non-verbal Communication

Brimming with practical ideas you can try today, *The Elusive Obvious* reveals the twenty-one non-verbals that are found at the heart of all communication models, no matter how different they may appear on the surface.

Easy to read and understand, this ground-breaking book explores the roots and mastery of non-verbal behaviors that make up 90% of all communication. The non-verbals presented form the foundation of influence and success in communication.

Written as a blend of textbook and instruction manual, *The Elusive Obvious* is a resource for trainers, managers, students, teachers, and researchers in non-verbal communication.

The Elusive Obvious is the compilation of Michael Grinder's 40 years of observational research on four continents. Book. $34.95

The Elusive Obvious DVD

Each Pentimento pattern and How Not to Get Shot! component is explained and demonstrated on 60 minutes of video footage. This DVD is designed to teach people how to deliver volatile information while preserving the relationship. DVD. $49.95

The Elusive Obvious Laminates

Five 5½" x 8½" color-coded pages summarize the Pentimento patterns and How Not to Get Shot! components. The lamination makes them an especially durable tool to remind the learner to use the skills. $9.95

The Elusive Obvious Flash Cards

The twenty-one Pentimento patterns and eight How Not to Get Shot! components have been produced in a deck of full-color, plastic-coated cards (the size of a standard deck of playing cards). Each card highlights a different pattern or component with written explanations and accompanying illustrations. Their mobile size makes them great for use at important interactions and reinforcing the ideas you've been learning. (Created by Isabel Azevedo and Kari Kvaerner.) $9.95

The Elusive Obvious Album

Includes all of The Elusive Obvious products in one attractive case: Book, DVD, Laminates and Flash Cards, plus a bonus CD of the worksheets. $89.95

Managing Groups

Michael Grinder has published his seminal work on group dynamics—*Managing Groups*. The book has two versions: *The Inside Track* is 500 pages and is the choice of those versed with his work.

The Fast Track is 250 pages and is popular amonst people who want to familiarize themselves with his work.

Managing Groups—The Inside Track From Good to Great is filled with Michael Grinder's wisdom into the inside workings of group dynamics. Based on his forty-years' experience in training and coaching thousands of groups, *Managing Groups—The Inside Track From Good To Great* identifies why groups do what they do and provides a solid, step-by-step system to build and sustain successful, thriving groups. $49.95

Managing Groups—The Fast Track gives the busy professional the "Cliff Notes" to group dynamics success based on Michael Grinder's forty-years' experience compiled in his integral work Managing Groups—The Inside Track. The Fast Track buides the reader with simple, clear processes to build trust and relationships that sustain successful groups. $34.95

Amazing Face Reading

Face reading is a means to a deeper communication with every person you meet. Fulfer takes this art/science out of the realm of the mysterious and into a hands-on method of learning. The most comprehensive, easy-to-use book of Face Reading available today. Amazing Face Reading is organized in an encyclopedic format and superbly illustrated. It takes you through faces, top to bottom, detail to gestalt, gesture to metaphoric meaning. This how-to guide is so easy to use that you can begin to read faces before you finish the book. $17.95

Charisma—The Art of Relationships

Why are some people easy to influence and work with and others are not? *Charisma—The Art of Relationships* delightfully answers this question and instructs how to increase your charisma. Using the analogy of house pets, this work provides methods to help you:

- Understand and accept yourself and others
- Separate your and others' intention from actions
- Interpret your and others' behaviors more accurately
- Increase resolving conflicts and knowing which conflicts not to try to resolve
- Improve your leadership skills and manage difficult personalities

The concepts are highlighted with icons in the margins indicating that a worksheet has been developed to practice the skill. Over 100 worksheets have been created which are available free at www.michaelgrinder.com.

This paperback book is 5½" x 8½" with 144 pages. Its compact size allows the reader to carry it anywhere. Book: $13.95.

Charisma Worksheets and Screen Savers

We are all very busy and yet want to continue to professionally grow. Screen savers address this need. When our computers are at rest, the concepts appear on the screen with an attractive background. The page reference is listed to encourage us to further extend our learning. Free downloads at www. michaelgrinder.com.

Charisma—The Art of Relationships
Live from London, DVD and Audio Album

Spend 1-1/2 hours with Michael as he entertainingly applies his cat and dog analogy to a wide array of applications. Topics include raising teenagers, understanding how to manage difficult personalities, increasing the efficiency of committee meetings and developing presentation skills. Michael's engaging style, humorous anecdotes and poignant insights will have you both laughing and reflecting at the same time. DVD & Audio Album: $49.95. (Album includes a Bonus CD of Charisma Worksheets and Screen Savers.) Also sold separately. DVD: $39.95; Audio CD: $19.95.

Tear Soup by Pat Schweibert and Chuck DeKlyen

Tear Soup, a recipe for healing after loss, is a family story book. It recognizes and reinforces the fact that every member of the family from the youngest to the oldest will grieve in their own way. Taking their own time and in doing so, find those things which help them best. Essentially, we each make our own batch of Tear Soup when we grieve the loss of someone we love or for any major change in our lives. By emphasizing the individual process of bereavement by making soup, Grandy's brings a warm and comfortable feeling to an otherwise difficult subject matter for many individuals. Book: $19.95

You Just Don't Understand by Deborah Tannen

Women and men live in different worlds...made of different words. This is the book that brought gender differences in ways of speaking to the forefront of public awareness. With a rare combination of scientific insight and delightful, humorous writing, Tannen shows why women and men can walk away from the same conversation with completely different impressions of what was said. Studded with lively and entertaining examples of real conversations, this book gives you the tools to understand what went wrong—and to find a common language in which to strengthen relationships at work and at home. Book $14.00

Ungame: Rhea Zakich

The Ungame is a board game that, as the name implies, is not intended for competition for but communication. The author, at one time in her life, was unable to talk. After meals of mostly silence, she wrote cards with questions on them and placed them at her family's plates. The circle of communication was revived. In time she became so comfortable with her temporary affliction that she resumed giving dinner parties. Her guests had such a great time that they encouraged her to publish the product; hence, the board game. The board game comes with generic questions. The two decks we carry are for couples and for family. Couples Cards: $9.00; Family Cards: $9.00

Classroom Management Trilogy

After 17 years of teaching experience on three levels of education, Michael visited 6,000 classrooms. He wanted to find out, "What do the most effective teachers have in common?" From these visitations, he identified the patterns that were almost universally seen in high-quality learning environments. He formulated what he observed into clear and easily learned management strategies, sorted them into three major categories, and published the results in this trilogy:

- *A Cat In The Dog House*—How to establish relationships with the hard-to-reach students.
- *ENVoY*—How to preserve the relationships while managing. Book, DVD, Pamphlets, Inservice Kit.
- *A Healthy Classroom*—How to utilize relationships between the students—group dynamics.

Successful management is based on a positive working relationship between the teacher and the students. Michael's products and trainings are based on the following axiom:

We are inadvertently in love with the influence of *Power*
We need to be in love with the power of *Influence*.

Visit our website for:

- Free downloadable screen savers for *Charisma— The Art of Relationships* and *A Healthy Classroom*.

- Free downloadable worksheets

- Schedule of Michael's classes

- List of educational recognized ENVoY trainers and their class schedules

- Free email quote of the day sign up

- Latest announcements

- Additional products

www.michaelgrinder.com

MGA PRODUCT ORDER FORM

Title	Unit	Qty	Total
The Elusive Obvious by Michael Grinder			
The Elusive Obvious (The Science of Non Verbal Communication). Book	34.95		
The Elusive Obvious DVD	49.95		
The Elusive Obvious Book and DVD	69.95		
The Elusive Obvious Laminates	9.95		
The Elusive Obvious Flash Cards	9.95		
The Elusive Obvious Album. Includes Book, DVD, Laminates, Flash Cards and Bonus CD of Worksheets	89.95		
The Elusive Obvious ebook	15.95		
Charisma by Michael Grinder			
Charisma—The Art of Relationships. Book. 10% discount on orders of 10 to 19; 20% discount on orders of 20 or more.	13.95		
Charisma—The Art of Relationships, Live from London, DVD	39.95		
Charisma—The Art of Relationships, Live from London, Audio CD	19.95		
Charisma—The Art of Relationships, Live from London, DVD & Audio Album (Worksheets and Screen Savers Bonus CD)	49.95		
Charisma—The Art of Relationships, ebook	9.95		
Charisma—The Art of Relationships. Cat & Dog Profile	7.50		
Managing Groups by Michael Grinder			
Managing Groups—The Fast Track. Book	34.95		
Managing Groups—The Inside Track. Book	49.95		
Managing Groups—The Fast Track, ebook	15.95		
Managing Groups—The Fast Track, Interactive ebook	21.95		
Managing Groups—The Inside Track, ebook	25.95		
Elusive Obvious and *Fast Track* ebook bundle	25.95		
Elusive Obvious, Fast Track and *Charisma* ebook super bundle	32.95		
Classroom Management Trilogy by Michael Grinder			
ENVoY: Your Personal Guide to Classroom Management. Book. Bulk discount on 10 or more	32.95		
ENVoY Seven Gems DVD	49.95		
ENVoY Book and Seven Gems DVD	71.95		
ENVoY Seven Gems Pamphlets (set of 7) 10% discount on orders of 10 to 19; 20% discount on orders of 20 or more.	5.00		
ENVoY The Seven Gems In-service Kit	295.00		
ENVoY: Your Personal Guide to Classroom Management, ebook	25.95		
A Healthy Classroom. Book. 40% discount on 10 or more	34.95		

Title	Unit	Qty	Total
A Healthy Classroom, ebook	25.95		
ENVoY and *A Healthy Classroom* ebook bundle	47.95		
ENVoY, *A Healthy Classroom*, and *Charisma* ebook super bundle	55.95		
Righting The Educational Conveyor Belt. Book. Bulk discount on 10 or more	23.95		
Righting The Educational Conveyor Belt, ebook	14.95		
Educational CDs on the At-risk, Building Relationships, Avoiding Escalations & Confrontations. 3 CDs	19.95		
Fundamentals of Group Dynamics CDs: How Not to Get Shot!, Handling Attacks, Overcoming Resistance. 3 CDs	59.95		
Other Corporate Products			
Amazing Face Reading, Mac Fulfer	17.95		
You Just Don't Understand, Deborah Tannen. Men and women conversation styles.	14.00		
The Really Good Fun Cartoon Book of NLP, Philip Miller	18.95		
Home Products			
Tear Soup; A Recipe For Healing After Loss, P. Schwiebert & C. DeKlyen	19.95		
The Ungame Couples Cards. Great conversation starters.	9.00		
The Ungame Family Cards	9.00		
Other Educational Products			
Thinklers, Kevin Brougher	16.50		
New Management Handbook, Rick Morris	20.00		

All prices subject to change.

Michael Grinder & Associates · 16303 N.E. 259th Street · Battle Ground, WA 98604
Phone: (360) 687-3238 · Fax (360) 687-0595
Website: www.michaelgrinder.com

Rev. 08/13